# rice pasta couscous

# rice pasta couscous

The Heart of the Mediterranean Kitchen

Lebanon · Turkey · Tunisia · Greece · Syria · Italy · Malta · Egypt · Croatia · France · Algeria · Morocco · Spain

**by Jeff Koehler**

Studio photographs by Sara Remington
Location photographs by Jeff Koehler

CHRONICLE BOOKS
SAN FRANCISCO

**For Alba and Maia, and, as always, Eva**

Library of Congress Cataloging-in-Publication Data available.

ISBN 978-0-8118-6297-4

Manufactured in China.

Design: Barretto-Co.
Food stylist: Erin Quon
Prop stylist: Kami Bremyer

10 9 8 7 6 5 4 3 2 1

Chronicle Books LLC
680 Second Street
San Francisco, California 94107

www.chroniclebooks.com

## Acknowledgments

During my research and travels for this book, I acted something like a jackdaw, collecting scraps of information in markets, fishing ports, restaurants, and kitchens around the Mediterranean. I do not know the names of many who generously shared their knowledge, but I do offer my sincere thanks to them.

Those that I can thank by name begin with my family north of Seattle, especially my parents Bill and Joanne who supported this book in many ways (even occasionally joining me on the road for it). Also, thanks to my grandparents, aunts and uncles, and brother, Bill, and his wife, Sarah. I am grateful to Tod Nelson, Jim Finley, Kirk Giloth, Robert Brown, and Caspar for their insight into the craft of writing, and to Kevin Miyazaki for his photography.

The roots of this book run deepest in Spain, and thanks there begin with my parents-in-law, Tomàs and Rosa, and sisters-in-law, Marien, Rosa María, and Carmina (and their supportive husbands). Also, thanks to Sanae Nouali and Sandra Martínez—las tías in Sinarcas—and their families; Natàlia Reixach and Jaime Pascual; Carl Gort and Montse Tarrús; Eli Jaso and Cesc Segura; Cristina Chiva and Dani Cárdena; my father-in-law's domino partners Pepe and Nicolás; Antoni Cot at Bouquet d'Aromes; Albert Asín at Bar Pinotxo; Santos Ruiz Álvarez; and Virginia Irurita and her staff at Made for Spain.

I would also like to single out the following for their significant help: with France—Valeria Judkowski and Pascal Poignard; Aicha Muniga; Simon Nataf; and Robert Bon. With Italy—Countess Rosetta Clara Cavalli d'Olivola and her son, Paolo, at Principato di Lucedio; Silvestro Angelo at Ristorante Balin; Francesca Marigliano; Vincenzo Giugliano and Heather Hartley; Carla Meucci; Eleonora Monti Gillen; Traci Woish; and Luca and Marie-Helen, the Counts Brondelli di Brondello. With Croatia—Nikola and Maria Vicelic; and Jen (Butorac) Straube. With Greece—Sylvia Gillis and Dora Zerwoodis. With Turkey—Mustafa Varoglu and his parents, Erol and Gonul; Batu Akyol; Ergin Sönmezler at Lokanta Yanyali; Aydin Gür at Sanat; and Vedat Basaran at Feriye Lokantasi. With Cyprus—Yiannakis Agapiou, president of the Cyprus Chef's Association. With Syria—Georges Husni, founding president of the Académie Syrienne de la Gastronomie. With Tunisia—Abderrazak Haouari and family; Habiba Abdelkéfi and family at Dar El Jeld. With Algeria—Sid Ali Lahlou and family at Maison Lahlou. And with Morocco—Philippe Guiguet-Bologne and Abdellatif at Dar Nour; and Louis Soubrier, Zohra, and Mustafa at BerBari.

Warm thanks to Naomi Duguid and Jeffrey Alford who continue to generously offer a stream of ideas, advice, and creative support.

Also thanks to the various editors who have supported—and honed—my writing and photography, including Dana Bowen, Paul Love, and James Oseland at *Saveur*, Jocelyn Zuckerman at *Gourmet*, Kate Heddings and Tina Ujlaki at *Food & Wine*, Michelle Wolfe at *Men's Journal*, Jeanne McManus at the *Washington Post*, Catharine Hamm and Craig Nakano at the *Los Angeles Times*, Jennifer Wolcott at *The Christian Science Monitor*, Allison Cleary and Patsy Jamieson at *EatingWell*, Michelle Wildgen at *Tin House*, Justin Paul and Marika Cain at *Virtuoso Life*, Michael Buller at *Continental*, and Paz Tintoré at *Foods from Spain News*.

For the beautiful photos of the finished dishes, thanks to Sara Remington and her crew—food stylist Erin Quon, prop stylist Kami Bremyer, food stylist assistant Vicki Woollard, and photo assistant Adi Nevo.

As always, deep-felt appreciation to my superb agent, Doe Coover, and those in her office, including Frances Kennedy.

At Chronicle Books, I would like to thank my editor, Amy Treadwell, who was a part of this project from the very beginning; her boss, Bill LeBlond; Sarah Billingsley, who helped shepherd it through the final stages; Vanessa Dina, for her designs; Emilia Thiuri, for her keen copyediting; managing editors, Ann Spradlin, Doug Ogan, and Elissa Bassist; publicity manager David Hawk; production coordinator, Michelle Clair; and marketing master, Peter Perez, for his enthusiasm. Also, thanks to Josh Rubinstein and Joseph Ternes for their work on my Web site, www.jeff-koehler.com. And to two others, not directly connected with this book, but very much part of my Chronicle family—Leslie Jonath and Alan Rapp.

And finally to my wife, Eva, and my two daughters, Alba and Maia—wonderful, patient companions on the road and faithful helpers in the kitchen—measuring, stirring, and, most important, tasting.

# CONTENTS

# PASTA

# COUSCOUS

## The Culture of Rice, Pasta, and Couscous in the Mediterranean

Around the Mediterranean, the soul is celebrated through the stomach. Food is a main ingredient of life, the center of nearly everything, and forms—with politics and soccer—the holy trinity of passions (and conversation topics).

The markets—from the splendid covered ones of Istanbul and Valencia to the sprawling souks of Fez and Cairo and Aleppo—are temples dedicated to the pursuit and pleasure of good food that is, undeniably, a daily priority, and they supply the ample bounty of products that define the region's magnificent cuisines.

At the heart of these various Mediterranean cuisines lies a trio of traditional staples that remain fundamental to today's diets: rice, pasta, and couscous. These three ingredients not only are present in day-to-day life as *alimentos básicos* but are also served when families gather for special meals to celebrate life's milestones and religious holidays: smoky, meat-and-rice-stuffed soured cabbage rolls (page 40) for Christmas Day on the Dalmatian coast, a vegetable-rich lamb couscous (page 176) served forty days after the death of a family member in Algiers. Although traditions vary from region to region and home to home, these staples are so deeply ingrained into their cultures, are so much a part of *la vie quotidienne*, that they have become symbols.

I have lived on the Mediterranean for more than a decade but have traveled the region for twenty years. I've explored virtually every corner of it, wandering lost in its ancient cities, haggling in its markets, crisscrossing its waves, and never once have I tired of its food-centered vitality. I remember my first trip so clearly, coming down out of the Swiss Alps through Italy to Rome and then Naples, fresh-faced, eighteen, and absorbing it all: the heaping bowls of pasta, the boisterous and cluttered food markets, the clatter of spoons frantically stirring tiny cups of espresso, the approach to food and the way of eating that seemed so different. We struck up a romance, the Mediterranean and me.

After graduating university, I spent four ambling years traveling. During that time, for me, food was as much a part of the joy and discovery as the people and places. I explored and ate my way through Africa, the Middle East, and Asia before settling in London to do graduate work. There, in a shared Hampstead residence-hall kitchen, I met a Catalan woman named Eva. When she returned home to Barcelona, I followed. We married a year later and, for most of the past twelve years, have lived here.

It was around Eva's parents' table that I began to understand just how deeply ingrained food was into Catalan culture. My mother-in-law Rosa's weekly paella is a family event. (A comfort, not an obligation.) She has been preparing one almost every weekend since getting married in the early 1960s. At first it was the newlyweds' parents who came, different aunts and distant cousins, and, before long, four daughters were sitting around the table, too. Eventually came boy-friends, husbands, grandchildren. Everything, it seems, passes through these weekend gatherings, from books being recommended to new jobs and engagement an-nouncements. Indeed, it was over one such paella that I cleared my throat and expressed, in a well-rehearsed sentence, Eva's and my desire to marry and, some years later with equal nervousness over an almost identical lunch, that we announced that we were expecting our first daughter.

Over countless plates of Rosa's sumptuous seafood paella, I learned not only how a simple staple could be trans-formed into something sublimely delicious, but how it can anchor both family and community. So enamored was I by the concept, that I wrote an entire book about it called *La Paella: Deliciously Authentic Rice Dishes from Spain's Mediterranean Coast* with Rosa's signature paella at its core.

The family lunches and the book also acted as stepping-stones to a broader Mediterranean picture. I traveled widely around the region and to such disparate places as Vercelli and Algiers, Tangier and Split, Palermo and Alexandria, and Tunis and Marseille, and I began to see more and more the similarities between the role of rice in my life and the role of rice, pasta, or couscous in others' lives. I saw that friends in North Africa gathered at their mothers' homes for boisterous lunches of couscous after midday Friday prayers and shared the week's events just as we did on Saturdays over rice and just as other friends in Italy did on Sundays over huge meals that always featured plenty of pasta. The similarities were striking.

The Mediterranean can be roughly divided by which of these three staples dominates an area. Broadly speaking, rice is the prevalent staple along the Spanish Mediterra-nean coast in Valencia, Catalonia, Murcia, and Alicante; in northern Italy, especially in parts of Piedmont and Lombardy; along Croatia's Dalmatian coast; and in the eastern Mediterranean, namely Greece, Turkey, Cyprus, Syria, Lebanon, Egypt, and the eastern half of Libya. Pasta reigns across most of Italy (as a friend's mother in Naples put it, "A meal isn't considered a meal without pasta"), but also in Malta and on Croatia's Istrian Pen-insula. And couscous is so much the dominant staple in the Maghreb—Morocco, Algeria, Tunisia, and western Libya—that some there call it, simply, *ta'am*, or "food."

Across these spheres of dominance, the cultural impor-tance of rice, pasta, and couscous, as well as their uses in the kitchen and role on the table, often run parallel. In this book, details on regional varieties, different flavors, and diverse methods of preparations will come later, in the "Primers" for each section, before the recipes. First, I want to dwell a bit on their stories that are, so frequently, the same.

. . .

For centuries rice, pasta, and couscous have offered cooks a staple substance, a healthful, highly nutritive base on which to build countless meals. They're inex-pensive. They're starchy and filling (and for the modern consumer, low fat and cholesterol free). They store well for long-term presentation. And they offer unparalleled versatility in the kitchen.

In the eastern Mediterranean, seasoned rice is packed into vegetables but also into capons and lamb in Greece, calamari in Crete, mussels in Turkey (page 38), and grape leaves just about everywhere. My favorite version of the last one is from Egypt, where the rolls tend to be smaller, like stubby fingers, singing with lemon and dipped into thick, mint-flaked yogurt. In Egypt I also savored rice-stuffed pigeons (page 82), delighting in

sucking the last of the meat off bones as fine as toothpicks, and, in northern Morocco, fish marinated in *charmoula* sauce, loosely filled with rice and large purplish olives, and baked to juicy perfection (page 85). Studded with dried fruits and nuts, couscous also makes superb stuffing, especially in chickens (page 189), pigeons, and quail.

Added to soups, rice and small pasta shapes make more substantial, filling dishes—a handful of rice into egg-lemon soup (page 47) in Athens or vermicelli noodles crumbled into lentil *chorba* (page 104) on a cold night in Algiers. *Sopa* in Barcelona means long-simmering meats and vegetables to draw out their flavor, removing them, and then boiling pasta in the rich broth. At home we eat lots of sopa, sometimes three or four times a week, thanks to our six-year-old daughter, Alba, who asks for it daily—I don't exaggerate. Her four favorite dishes are, in this order, sopa with short thin pasta, sopa with star-shaped pasta, sopa with letter-shaped pasta, and sopa with pine nut–shaped pasta. Ask what she wants for dinner, and the answer is, without fail, "Sopa!"

For dessert, versions of sweet, chewy rice puddings appear all around the Mediterranean, from creamy Greek *rizogalo* with vanilla and whisked egg (page 87) to oven-baked Turkish *sütlaç*, flavored with mastic (page 88). The aromatics of rice puddings may change with the location, but the rich, milky sweetness remains constant. In our home we love sweetened couscous trimmed with dates and nuts (page 205) and served with glasses of cold milk. Recently this has been threatened by a new favorite, Moroccan *seffa chariya*, short thin noodles double-steamed in the *couscoussier* and dusted with confectioners' sugar and cinnamon.

Mostly, though, rice, pasta, and couscous are the basis of a meal's principal dish, combinable with just about every level of expense, flavor, and sophistication.

A thrifty cook in Tangier might prepare couscous with the week's leftover vegetables, while an extravagant one in Mallorca might use spiny lobsters in soupy rice.

The peak of simplicity and extravagance, which I first savored in the *enoteca* of a tiny, unfashionable Piedmont hill town, is fresh tagliatelle pasta with white truffles shaved over the top (page 111). It's a dish not so much to die for, but to kill for. (The sea equivalent is *spaghetti ai ricci di mare*—spaghetti with sea urchin. Divine!)

The mild taste of these bases means that they can be eaten quite simply and "every day"—a "sauceless" couscous with fresh peas in Algiers (page 173), Greek orzo pasta with brown butter and aged kasseri cheese (page 144)—or else draw on the region's seasonal bounty.

Last autumn, the family gathered for my in-laws' forty-fifth wedding anniversary at a weekend country house, a sturdy, century-old place with a great peaked slate roof. In the market, I bought three types of just-arrived wild mushrooms—*camagrocs* (golden-yellow trumpet-shaped "yellow legs"), *trompetes de la mort* (deep black and musky "trumpets of death"), and *rovellons* (meaty and orange)—and in the small kitchen lined with original, antique tiles, prepared these splendid seasonal offerings in a soupy rice with duck for twenty of us. The fall day was sunny and crisp, and we sat around a single long table outside, the adults lingering over coffee long after the kids—aged three to twenty-three—had dispersed in search of pinecones to crack open for the nuts inside.

For such family meals, these staples frequently form the centerpiece; the concept of extended families gathering for a regular weekend meal remains strong. Whereas my mother-in-law prepares paella, other friends prepare *fideuà*, essentially paella made with short, thin fideo noodles instead of rice (page 139). These types of dishes are perfect for such gatherings. To start with, neither couscous, paella, nor fideuà is ever prepared for just one or two people. That concept simply doesn't exist. Traditionally, a large platter mounded with couscous is set down among extended family and friends, the guests getting the choicest bits of lamb or chicken. Paella has that same communal sense when being eaten directly from the pan. This is the rustic face of Spain's emblematic

dish, which has its roots in farmers who could not make it back home for lunch from the *huertas*—the abundant produce gardens outside Valencia—where they worked. They cooked vegetables (and, if they were lucky, a rabbit or duck they had shot) with the rice over the cuttings of pruned trees, and then clustered around and ate it directly from the pan with spoons.

...

On a cultural level, rice, pasta, and couscous offer an identity to whole swaths of the Mediterranean. In the Maghreb, couscous marks every step of life from birth to death. "Couscous is our *patrimoine*," Sid Ali Lahlou, an Algerian Berber, restaurateur, and couscous producer, told me (see "Primary Source: Sid Ali Lahlou," page 181). Like many Berbers, his family celebrates every special event and significant occasion with mounds of couscous. "You can make different dishes, but couscous is obligatory."

At similar occasions in the eastern Mediterranean, it's rice that's always present. In Turkey, *iç pilav*, pilaf with liver, pine nuts, and currants (page 76), is prepared for a handful of guests as well as the largest, most important gatherings, including weddings and boys' circumcision parties. In Lebanon and Syria, families prepare *moghli*, an aromatic rice-flour pudding seasoned with caraway, anise, and plenty of cinnamon (page 89), for guests to celebrate the birth of a baby.

Many Christmas lunches in northern Italy begin with tortellini (or cappelletti) in capon broth (page 108), while Catalan Christmas lunches mean a fuller version of sopa with large pasta shells called *galets de Nadal* (page 106). The day after Christmas, Sant Esteban, is a day with equally important family gatherings, and any leftover meat from making Christmas Day's soup broth is ground and used to stuff cannelloni. These days there seems to be little of that meat left over (at least in our family), so my mother-in-law cooks more the next morning and then grinds it by hand. While the twenty or more of us belly up to the table and begin working on the vast array of *pica-pica* (appetizers)—dates wrapped in bacon and then fried, thin slices of fat-marbled cured ham, and grilled local prawns—she slides trays filled with cannelloni into the oven for a gratin and then carries them out to cheers.

Orthodox Greeks (more than 95 percent of the population of Greece belongs to the Greek Orthodox Church) and Cypriots (who make up the southern two-thirds of Cyprus) have long periods of fasting—the forty-day Lenten period, as well as from November 15 to December 24, and every Wednesday and Friday—when they cannot eat ingredients from animals with blood (no meat, eggs, milk, butter, chicken stock). Rice and greens form a major part of the diet during these times, and believers eat vast quantities of stuffed vegetables, pilafs, and homey *spanakorizo* (spinach with rice, page 77). For Easter, the most important celebration of the Orthodox calendar, a lamb is slaughtered. The offal goes into a rice-filled soup, *mayiritsa*, served after the midnight liturgy to break the fast, and the lamb is spit roasted for the main Easter Sunday meal.

For the Muslim Mediterranean, one of the most important times of the year is Ramadan, a month when all consumption of food and drink is forbidden between sunrise and sunset. Fasting is one of the five pillars of Islamic faith, and the abstinence shows obedience to Allah and atonement for sins and errors. The feeling of hunger is a reminder of the suffering of the less fortunate.

A few winters ago, I was on the southern Tunisian island of Jerba during Ramadan. I remember arriving in the center of the main city, Houmt Souk, late in the afternoon, as people were scrambling to buy last-minute items as shopkeepers were desperately trying to shutter up. The manager of a small *fondouk* handed me my room key and quickly disappeared into the kitchen behind the breakfast nook. I climbed up to the roof and looked out over the empty streets. The call to prayer sounded from a minaret nearby, and then another, and another, and across the low cityscape the tinny, passionate, and melodic prayer echoed, followed by a resounding "Boom!" marking the end of the fast. The city fell into pure silence. A moment later I smelled the cigarette smoke from the manager's quarters below, followed by laughter and the clanking of spoons. When the streets eventually refilled and the cafes reopened, I went down for dinner. I was hungry, and on that wet, windy night, a nourishing bowl of *sherba*, a thick soup rich with tomatoes, lamb, and small pasta, spritzed with lemon and spiced with a dollop of harissa chile paste, was just right.

The next winter when I returned to Jerba, Ramadan had not long finished, and over lunch with the family of the great Tunisian chef Abderrazak Haouari (see "Primary Source: Abderrazak Haouari," page 202), the children gleefully recited for me their typical *iftar* meal, still so fresh in their minds: first dates and coffee with milk, then sherba, salad, *brik* (a triangular fried pastry filled with, among other things, a runny egg), and then couscous or a big plate of spaghetti with spicy tomato sauce. For them, Ramadan is a time of celebration, of long meals and special foods.

A month after Ramadan is another important Muslim festival, Eid al-Adha, the Festival of Sacrifice. To commemorate Ibrahim's (Abraham's) willingness to sacrifice his son Isaac to Allah, as well as marking the end of the Hajj, the annual pilgrimage to Mecca, sheep are slaughtered. One winter, I was in Algiers during the final lead-up to the celebration. The markets and many street corners were lively in anticipation of the feast to come. Huddling over morning coffees in the smoky Brasserie des Facultés along rue Didouche Mourad and afternoon glasses of murky, sweet tea on Café Tontonville's broad terrace at the end of Place Port Saïd, I saw chunky rams with curling horns being hustled through the busy boulevards by young kids, long sticks in hand, laughing. Within days they would be butchered and eaten with great mounds of fluffy couscous.

During Ramadan in Turkey, rice takes a public face when the municipality erects tents around the city and serves free pilaf with chickpeas. In a similar, though nonreligious, vein, many neighborhoods or towns along the Spanish Mediterranean prepare large paellas that feed hundreds. Every October in my Barcelona neighborhood, a handful of volunteers set up long tables in a small square, covering them in paper and lining them with bottles of red wine, as other volunteers prepare different paellas. Last autumn, Alba and I walked up to a nearby square for chicken and seafood paella for 500 people (cooked in a single, enormous pan!), a luncheon organized by the Catalan Socialist party. It was during regional elections, and the "ticket" was free—but first you had to listen to the presidential candidate speak!

In Valencia there are no shortages of paella contests, from the dozens held in neighborhoods during the raucous Las Falles celebration to the annual fifty-year-old paella contest in Sueca, on the southern fringe of the Albufera rice fields. Farther down the coast, there is a well-known fideuà contest in Gandia and another long-running one in Dénia for *arròs a banda* (similar to paella, but the rice and the fish are served seperately). San Vito lo Capo, an isolated town on the northwest corner of Sicily, hosts an international couscous festival every year in September with chefs representing the couscous-eating countries competing for top honors.

Such contests are an opportunity to show off an expert's touch, and rice, pasta, and couscous have long been ideal modeling clay for culinary artistry. In the mid-17th century, the Ottoman royal kitchens in Istanbul had a live-in staff of 1,375. With virtually every ingredient at their disposal, from nuts and butter to expensive saffron, chefs took pilafs to dizzying heights of refinement and complexity. Morocco, too, had—has!—royalty that supported a court cuisine, and in the imperial kitchens of Marrakech, Fez, Meknès, and Rabat, couscous hits similar high notes of sophistication and decadence. On the palace grounds in Rabat, a royal cooking school teaches young women to prepare the classic dishes. They do not use written recipes but must prepare the dishes over and over again until perfected. Such skills

were once the mark of womanhood around the Mediterranean: I've read that Turkish women in Ottoman times were adept at making twenty-seven different types of pilafs and Calabrian women were ready to wed only once they mastered at least twelve different pasta shapes.

These days, Spanish chefs are pushing hardest against culinary limits. There is Ferran Adrià and his alchemy, of course, but when I think of breathtaking, original rices, I think of a handful of inventive young chefs in Valencia. At the top are Raúl Aleixandre at Ca' Sento working with, simply, the finest ingredients from his stretch of coastline, and at El Poblet in Dénia, Quique Dacosta, who recently garnered a second Michelin star for his daring, free-floating gastronomic masterpieces that look more like landscapes than lunch! But perhaps the finest rice I've ever eaten was prepared by (the even younger) Josep Quintana at Torrijos in downtown Valencia, a spectacular moist rice with partridge, foie gras, and the smoke of burned acorn twigs. Sublime.

Around our table, though, my girls want more straightforward cooking: a fish couscous with plenty of broth, a risotto creamy with butter and Parmigiano-Reggiano, handmade pasta. These are dishes they love but also can help prepare. "What can I do?" Alba begs, and her younger sister, Maia, responds to every direction with "Me, also!" They stand beside me on stools, in their brightly patterned aprons sewn by their great-grandmother, and rub grains of couscous between their small palms or help make the pasta, one turning the handle on the machine, the other catching cut strands of tagliatelle sliding out.

The girls, not surprisingly, eat these meals with particular gusto. We discuss their day at school, an upcoming excursion, or the latest song in music class. News of jobs and boyfriends (and the boyfriends themselves!) will come one day. But I can wait for that, content for now to listen to the small details of their lives as they devour the food before them, the rice, pasta, or couscous that is at the center of our family table, and our life.

...

A note on spelling: Writing Arabic words in the Roman alphabet generates numerous problems, and there is little agreement in the international community about which spelling system to follow. My approach here lies not in a rigorous linguistic method; rather, I have used the variation that I have most frequently come across on packaging and in cookbooks and writing. I have retained certain French spellings, like *chorba* or *charmoula*, which have become quite standard in English. In North Africa, recipes names in most local cookbooks and menus are translated from Arabic into French (not phonetically written Arabic); I have done the same in English here.

# rice

# Mediterranean Rice Primer

## Brief History and Overview

Originating in East Asia, rice—*Oryza sativa*—has been cultivated for at least 7,000 years. Rice had a long trek west via India and arrived in the Mediterranean in two different prongs.

The Greeks introduced rice into Egypt, probably in the 7th century. By the 10th century it was an important Egyptian crop, which it remains today (second only to cotton in exportation). Along with some plantings in the oasis of Fayyum, rice is cultivated across the Nile Delta. This triangular region, reaching north of Cairo to the Mediterranean and measuring 109 miles long and 162 miles wide, is one of the most fertile places on Earth. From the days of the Pharaohs until the 19th century, Egyptians practiced basin irrigation every August and September when the Nile flooded its banks. Various dams and canals, and then the construction of the Aswan High Dam in the 1960s, eliminated seasonal irrigation and allowed the land to be cultivated on a larger scale. Planting mostly short- and medium-grain varieties, Egypt is the largest rice producer in the Near East, producing more than double that of the entire European Union. It grows more than it can consume and exports the remainder. Historically, only those people living along the Mediterranean Sea ate rice, but in 1968 the government gave each person 1 kilogram (2.2 pounds) of rice as aid. Rice caught on across the country and domestic consumption has grown to one of the highest outside Asia.

Rice's second and more wide-spreading entrance into the Mediterranean came via the Persians, who carried it from India back to Persia, and then the Arabs, who carried it west from there, introducing it into Spain shortly after conquering the Iberian Peninsula in the 8th century. (The Spanish and Catalan words for *rice*—*arroz* and *arròs*, respectively—come from the Arabic *ar-ruzz*.)

The oldest and most traditional rice-growing region in Spain is just south of Valencia along the shores of the Albufera, a freshwater lagoon separated from the sea by a thin line of dunes. It's also Spain's most important rice-growing region, producing 20 percent of the country's rice. A regulatory board, Denominacíon de Origen Protegida (DOP), controls the rice's origin and varietal purity and monitors production and harvesting. Two other important Spanish-protected rice areas are the Ebro Delta on the southern edge of Catalonia, which has been growing rice since at least 1607, and the mountainous, inland fields of Calasparra, dating back to the 15th century. Cold moving water, as opposed to still water in Valencia and the Ebro Delta, feeds Calasparra's fields, making harder, more absorbent grains that many connoisseurs consider to be the finest grown.

In the 8th or 9th century, Arabs introduced rice into Sicily. It grew in the southeast of the island into the 18th century, though the country's main rice-producing area had moved north by the 15th century to the moist climate and flat, fertile plains of the Po River Valley just west of Milan. Italy produces almost two-thirds of Europe's rice and nearly all of it in this valley around Vercelli and Novara in Piedmont and Lomellina in

Lombardy. Tellingly, northern Italians eat, on average, twenty pounds of rice per person per year—three times more than southern Italians.

In the late 16th century, Italian rice stock was introduced into the French Camargue delta at the mouth of the Rhône River, in the southwest tip of Provence. (On the counsel of his trusted minister Sully, Henry IV ordered it planted on August 23, 1593.) The first significant plantings in the Camargue, though, didn't occur until the 19th century, and major commercialization didn't begin until World War II, when French ports were blocked and maritime traffic was minimal. The importance of the crop died away by the 1970s, but the 1980s saw a revitalization, with long-grain rice largely replacing short-grain varieties (long-grain rice now accounts for around 79 percent of Camargue rice), and the introduction of Camargue red rice, a natural cross of indigenous red rice with short-grain japonica. The Camargue is home to nearly all of the rice planted in France (some 20,000 hectares/49,400 acres), yet apart from rice pudding, there is little traditional rice cuisine in southern France; today it's eaten in the delta as an accompaniment and used in local versions of pilaf and paella.

The ancient Greeks knew of rice by the 3rd century but considered it an expensive import and used it for medicinal purposes. It has been cultivated for the past two centuries in the north of the country around Thessaloníki and Serres (near the borders with Bulgaria and Turkey), but its importance as a local crop came largely after World War II. Production and consumption (in soups, stuffings, pilafs, and puddings) continue to increase, though, as in France, short- and medium-grain varieties have been largely replaced with long-grain ones.

Rice has a long and regal pedigree in Turkey, where it was a key ingredient in the royal kitchens of the Ottoman Empire. Once only eaten by the wealthy or on special occasions, rice still retains its status as a symbol. Rice is produced chiefly in the northwestern Marmara and Thrace regions and in the Black Sea region. Turkey uses so much *pirinç* (rice) in dolmas, pilafs, and sweet puddings that it has to import (mostly from Egypt) its balance.

Elsewhere in the eastern Mediterranean, rice is not cultivated; Cyprus, Syria, and Lebanon import most of their rice from Turkey and Egypt, as well as some from Iran and Pakistan. Croatia imports most of its rice from Italy.

In North Africa, only Morocco cultivates rice, though in very limited amounts. While Egyptians today consume a whopping ninety-five pounds of rice per person per year, Moroccans eat just four pounds, perhaps the lowest in the world. Here, and elsewhere in the Maghreb, rice is used to thicken soups, as stuffing, and as an accompaniment to other dishes.

## Key Varieties of Mediterranean Rice

The two major groups of rice cultivated in the Mediterranean are shorter, more glutinous japonica types, which originated in Japan and Korea, and longer indica types, which came from India, China, and Indonesia. Generally speaking, long-grain rice is more than three times longer in length than width, medium grain between two and three times longer, and short grain (sometimes also called round grain) less than two times longer. The following varieties are short- or medium-grain unless otherwise noted.

**ARBORIO:** Perhaps the best known Italian variety abroad (it was the first to be massively exported), Arborio's high degree of starch gives off a lovely creaminess during cooking. Excellent for risottos and desserts.

**BAHÍA:** A classic Spanish medium-grain rice with high absorption capabilities.

**BALDO:** One of the main varieties grown in Egypt and Turkey, Turkish cooks prefer Baldo for pilafs and sometimes use cut or broken Baldo grains (know as *kırık*) in dolmas and puddings. In Italy, where it's a relative newcomer, Baldo is emerging as a favorite because of its versatility and strong grains that don't break easily. Best served a little underdone in risottos.

**BALILLA:** The small, rounded grains of this Spanish and Italian variety are perfect in soups, rice puddings, and moist Spanish-style rices.

**BOMBA:** Firm and highly absorbent, Bomba is Spain's most famous (and expensive) rice and, until recently, was the only Valencian variety exported to North America. Bomba doesn't split lengthwise but rather unfolds accordion-like, expanding two or three times its length when cooked. Bomba holds its consistency longer and better resists overcooking than other Spanish short- or medium-grain varieties.

**CAMARGUE RED RICE:** *Riz rouge de Camargue* is a cross between an indigenous red rice and cultivated white short-grain japonica. The grains remain firm and not too sticky, and the flavor is pleasingly nutty. To cook, boil in abundant salted water for 40 minutes, drain, and eat as an accompaniment to fish, meat, or poultry.

**CARNAROLI:** Italy's grandest rice, and for risotto, simply the best. The bulky, creamy grains are superabsorbent while holding their shape and texture. Like Bomba, Carnaroli is comparatively resistant to overcooking.

**ROMA:** These are big, rounded, and starchy grains that are a good option for risottos.

**ROCCO:** The most widely grown rice in the Marmara and Thrace regions of Turkey.

**SANT'ANDREA:** Until recently sold under the name Rizzotto, Sant'Andrea was renamed after the cathedral in Vercelli, the city at the center of Italy's rice production. The grains are slightly smaller, with less starch than other similar Italian varieties. Ideal in soups and desserts.

**SENIA:** Very similar to Bahía, these versatile and highly absorbent grains are perfectly suited for traditional Valenciana rices.

**THAIBONNET:** An excellent long-grain variety grown in Italy and Greece. The long, narrow, and pointy grains are ideal for pilafs.

**VIALONE NANO:** The short, stocky, and almost round grains have a super-high level of absorption and need to cook a little longer than similar rices. It's the preferred variety for Veneto-style moist risottos. One of Italy's finest varieties.

**YASMINE:** A long-grain aromatic rice widely grown in Egypt.

**YPSALA:** A long-grain variety widely grown in Turkey.

## Spanish-Style Rices

Rice here is the protagonist and everything is done to give it flavor. The absorbent grains simply act as vehicles for flavor, soaking up the seasonings and stock in the pan.

Spanish rices can be divided by their levels of "dryness" and by the pans in which they are cooked. At the driest end are classic paellas, while moister rices are prepared in wide *cazuelas* (casseroles). When you need a spoon to eat the rice, it's called *caldoso* (from *caldo*, or "broth").

## Techniques and Secrets

### PANS AND UTENSILS

Spanish rice dishes frequently take the name of the pan in which they are prepared. A paella is called a paella because that's the name of the pan. A paella's wide, flat shape allows for maximum evaporation and as much rice as possible coming in contact with the bottom of the pan, where the flavors lie. The rice spreads into a thin layer—usually no more than 3/4 inch deep (I have eaten plenty of very wide-pan paellas in Valencia where the rice is only a few grains deep); to feed more people, the pan simply gets wider. Some common sizes are 14-inch pan for 3 to 4 people, 16-inch for 4 to 5, 18-inch for 5 to 6, 20-inch for 6 to 8, and 22-inch for 10. When all of the uncooked ingredients fill the pan, the liquid should reach the level of the handles.

In order to quickly respond to changes of heat, a paella pan needs to be made of thin, conductive metal. The most classic (and least expensive) is polished carbon steel, which also gives the rice a lovely, sweet tang. Carbon-steel pans need to be stored either rubbed with oil or dusted in flour. Stainless-steel pans are easier to maintain but are more expensive and are slightly slower to respond to change of heat. Enameled-steel pans are a good mid-range choice.

One or two large, lightweight sauté pans or skillets can substitute for a paella pan. For a paella for 4 to 6 people, use two 12-inch pans. Cook the meats and *sofrito* (vegetable base) together in one pan, transfer half to the second pan, and continue with the recipe. The classic *cazuela* (*cassola* in Catalan) is terra-cotta, though heavy aluminum and cast-iron versions are now widely used. Dutch ovens and large, heavy sauté pans or skillets make perfect alternatives.

### PREPARING PAELLA ON THE STOVE, FIRE, OR A GRILL

Paella's wide pan needs a wide, even source of heat. Special gas rings can be purchased (see Sources, page 211), but manipulating the kitchen stove works just fine: straddle the pan over three or even four burners and rotate it as the rice cooks. Preparing a paella over a live fire, preferably using vine cuttings, infuses the rice with delicious smoky hues. Though slightly less festive, a grill is easier and more controllable than live fire; use natural hardwood charcoal. Begin the process inside on the stove, cooking the meats and sofrito in a sauté pan or skillet before transferring to a paella pan set over the flames or the hot embers. Add the liquid, bring to a rolling boil, and add the rice. Be sure that the grill rack is level; check before lighting by placing the empty pan on the grill and adding the oil.

### THE RIGHT RICE

The grains need to be highly absorbent while remaining firm. Any Spanish short- or medium-grain variety will work, though Bomba is the best choice, especially for a novice paella maker. Italian risotto rices also work well, especially the moister ones. Alternatively, use Japanese short-grain rice. Do not rinse the rice first. Do not use long-grain or parboiled rice.

### AMOUNTS

The standard amount is 1/2 cup (3 1/2 ounces; 100 grams) of rice per person for paellas and moist rice dishes and 1/3 cup per person for soupy rice dishes.

### SOFRITO

Most recipes from Spain's Mediterranean coast begin with a sofrito (*sofregit* in Catalan), an aromatic, slow-cooked flavor base that usually includes onions and tomatoes, sometimes garlic, and occasionally green or red bell peppers. The slower a sofrito is cooked, the richer and more body it will have. Don't rush it! As my mother-in-law says, "A quick sofrito does not exist."

### STOCK

For Spanish-style rices (as well as risottos), a flavorful stock is key. Simply put, the better the stock, the better the rice.

### STIRRING (OR NOT!)

In a paella, once the rice has been added and probed to make sure that it's evenly distributed and under the surface of the liquid, it is never stirred. Never! Moister rice dishes, though, are stirred from time to time.

### PICADA

A *picada* is a pounded paste—usually of almonds, garlic, and parsley, plus maybe a bit of fried bread—that is stirred in at the end of many Catalan dishes, including moist rice ones, though never paellas. Picada gives structure and acts as a thickener but should be noticeable only for its earthy shading of flavors.

### RESTING

Paellas need to be covered with paper towels or a clean kitchen towel and rested in the pan for 5 minutes to finish cooking the top layers of rice and to firm up the starches. Moist cazuela rices should be dished up immediately and rested on the plate.

## Risotto

Risottos are defined by their creamy texture, chewy, firm grains, and general simplicity—an Italian onion *soffritto*, some herbs, a main ingredient or two (asparagus, perhaps mushrooms, or some shaved truffle). A knob of butter and grated Parmigiano-Reggiano are stirred in at

the last moment. Risottos in Veneto tend to be moister than those elsewhere in northern Italy.

### Techniques and Secrets

#### PANS AND UTENSILS

The ideal risotto pan is heavy and wide and has 4- to 5-inch-high sides. Pans sold as "risotto pans" and slightly round-bottomed sauciers work well. The only other tools needed are a good wooden spoon for the frequent stirring and a ladle for adding the broth.

#### THE RIGHT RICE

Starchy, highly absorbent rices, such as Carnaroli, Arborio, Vialone Nano, and, to a lesser extent, Baldo, make optimal choices for risottos. In northern Italy, risotto's main center, Carnaroli is considered to be the best. For moist, Veneto-style risottos, look for Vialone Nano. Do not rinse the rice first. Do not use long-grain or parboiled rice.

#### SOFFRITTO

The classic risotto has a slow-cooked flavor base of onion (or shallot) and sometimes garlic. It's important that the onions don't brown; adding a spoonful of stock to them as they cook helps keep them blond. (Soffrittos for pasta are usually more complex, and include tomatoes, sometimes celery, carrots, parsley, and even pancetta.)

#### TOASTING THE RICE

One of the first steps in preparing risotto is toasting the rice in the pan, just 3 to 4 minutes, until golden and nutty. Stir frequently to keep from scorching.

#### ADDING WINE AND STOCK

Adding dry white wine to the rice after toasting gives the risotto a characteristic clean and slightly tangy note. The wine should be gently warmed before adding it all at once. Hot stock is added ladleful by ladleful, waiting

for each to incorporate before adding the next. Small holes will appear in the surface of the rice and stirring will reveal just a hint of liquid on the bottom of the pan. If you run out of stock, finish with hot water. Canned stock needs to be thinned so that, as it reduces with cooking, the flavor does not overpower the rice.

### STIRRING
It's a myth that risottos need to be continually stirred. No less authority than Countess Rosetta Clara Cavalli d'Olivola, the proprietor of one of Italy's oldest and most prestigious rice farms, Principato di Lucedio, a woman who lives in the heartland of risotto and eats the dish two or three times a week (even more in the past), assured me that risotto only needs to be stirred enough to release the starch. It's sufficient to stir only with each addition of stock.

### OBTAINING CREAMINESS
One of the keys to risotto's creaming is the frequent stirring during cooking that slowly releases the soft starches surrounding rice kernels. The other key is adding butter and cheese at the end. (Too much will make it gummy.) Fresh, finely grated Parmigiano-Reggiano is the cheese of choice, though some cooks use Grana Padano (see page 99 for more on these cheeses). Cheese is not added to seafood risottos.

### RESTING AND SERVING
Rest the rice for 2 minutes before serving in warm bowls.

## Pilaf

Rice in Turkey is called *pirinç* though Turks tend to refer to the end product, the most important being pilav, or "pilaf." The grains of rice in a well-made pilaf are tender and fluffy, separate and shimmering with butter (or oil), and trickle off the spoon individually. Originating in Ottoman palace kitchens, pilaf dishes were carried by chefs throughout the empire and embedded into the cuisines of the entire eastern Mediterranean. Once served as a principal dish, pilaf often acts as a generous accompaniment.

### Techniques and Secrets
#### PANS AND UTENSILS
A large, heavy saucepan with a tight-fitting lid is essential. The typical pilaf spatula is wide and round with small holes that allow the rice to be turned over or served without breaking the grains.

#### THE RIGHT RICE
In Turkey, locally grown, medium-grain Baldo is the most popular choice for pilaf. I have found it is easier, though, to obtain perfect, separate grains in the style of Turkish pilafs with high-quality long-grain rice. Do not use parboiled rice.

#### RINSING AND SOAKING
Rinsing and soaking the rice before cooking removes the starches and helps keep the grains individual and separate during cooking. It also makes the grains less brittle and more resistant to breaking. Rinse the rice with plenty of changes of cool water until the water runs clear. Cover in warm salted water ($\frac{1}{2}$ teaspoon salt per 4 cups of water) and let sit until the water cools; rinse the rice in fresh water and drain through a sieve.

#### LIQUID
Purists use only water in their pilaf, but some cooks believe that a good stock makes more flavorful rice. (The recipes here all call for water.)

### COVERING AND STIRRING

Pilaf remains tightly covered while cooking. It is turned over gently, rather than stirred, only once (if at all) to ensure that the rice cooks evenly on the top and bottom of the pan.

### DRIED FRUITS AND NUTS

Currants—tiny, sweet dried grapes about the size of peppercorns—are the most typical dried fruit added to pilaf. Substitute roughly chopped seedless raisins. Pine nuts need to be dry roasted or fried in butter until golden to fully bring out their flavors before being gently folded into the rice.

### COVERING AND RESTING

After cooking, pilaf needs to rest and finish steaming off of the heat. Remove the lid of the pot, place a paper towel or clean kitchen towel tightly across it, and replace the lid snugly. Set the pot in a warm corner of the kitchen for an hour or so before serving.

## Stuffing

Throughout the eastern Mediterranean and the rest of the old Ottoman countries, from Algeria to Croatia, cooks stuff seasoned rice into just about everything that makes a packet: fish, lamb, squid, and every vegetable from squash blossoms to dried eggplant. The stuffing can be studded with pine nuts and currants and even include ground meat. In this part of the Mediterranean, meat usually means lamb, though beef works perfectly as well.

## Techniques and Secrets

### THE RIGHT RICE

Starchy short- or medium-grain rice keeps the stuffing together and best absorbs the flavors. Do not rinse the rice first. Do not use parboiled rice.

### PREPARING THE RICE

Rice is usually partially cooked with seasonings before being stuffed and finishes cooking in the oven or pot.

### YOGURT

There are two consistencies of yogurt in Turkey and Greece: a runny, unstrained version and a thicker, strained one. To make a thicker yogurt, secure a piece of cheesecloth over a bowl with kitchen twine, spoon in natural yogurt, and let the liquid (whey) drain for 1 to 2 hours. Discard the liquid and whisk the yogurt before using.

## Chicken Stock

| | | | | |
|---|---|---|---|---|
| 2 | pounds bone-in chicken meat, skin pulled off and fat trimmed | | 1 | celery rib, roughly chopped |
| | Salt and freshly ground pepper | | 10 | peppercorns |
| 1 | tablespoon extra-virgin olive oil | | 8 ½ | cups water |
| 1 | onion, roughly chopped | | 5 | sprigs fresh flat-leaf parsley, rinsed |
| 1 | leek, trimmed and roughly chopped | | 5 | sprigs fresh cilantro, rinsed |
| 1 | carrot, scrubbed and roughly chopped | | | |

Chop the chicken into chunks and season with salt and pepper.

In a stockpot or another large, heavy pot over medium heat, heat the oil. Add the chicken and cook until the pieces take a bit of color, about 5 minutes. Add the onion and cook until soft and golden, about 5 minutes. Add the leek, carrot, and celery and cook, stirring occasionally, until they begin to release their juices, about 5 minutes. Add the peppercorns and cover with the water. Bring to a boil, reduce the heat, cover, and simmer for 1 hour.

Remove from the heat. Add the parsley and cilantro, push them down into the liquid, and let infuse as the stock cools.

Strain the broth through a fine mesh sieve, gently pressing any remaining liquid from the chicken. Discard the solids.

If desired, cool the stock and skim off any fat that floats to the surface.

Store in the refrigerator for up to 3 or 4 days or freeze for longer.

## Fish Stock

Good fish for stock include scorpion fish, weaver fish, star-gazer, red mullet, red gurnard, and small conger eel. If you can't find these, look for monkfish heads or another firm white-fleshed fish, such as halibut, snapper, cod, or sea bass. Simmer them only long enough to poach their essence.

| | |
|---|---|
| 1 | tablespoon extra-virgin olive oil |
| 1 | Spanish onion, roughly chopped |
| | Salt |
| 1 | leek, trimmed and roughly chopped |
| 1 | carrot, scrubbed and roughly chopped |
| 1 | small turnip or parsnip, scrubbed and halved |
| 1 | celery rib, roughly chopped |

| | |
|---|---|
| 1 | tablespoon sweet pimentón (paprika) |
| 10 | peppercorns |
| 8 ½ | cups water |
| 2 | pounds assorted soup fish or the heads (gills removed) and bones of a flavorful firm, white-fleshed fish |
| 5 | sprigs fresh flat-leaf parsley, rinsed |
| 5 | sprigs fresh cilantro, rinsed |

In a stockpot or another large, heavy pot over medium heat, heat the oil. Add the onion and 2 generous pinches of salt and cook until soft and golden, about 5 minutes. Add the leek, carrot, turnip, and celery and cook, stirring occasionally, until they begin to release their juices, about 5 minutes. Add the pimentón and peppercorns and cover with the water. Bring to a low boil, and then add the fish. When the stock returns to a simmer, reduce the heat to low, partly cover, and simmer for 30 minutes.

Remove from the heat. Add the parsley and cilantro, push them down into the liquid, and let infuse as the stock cools.

Strain the broth through a fine mesh sieve, gently pressing any remaining liquid from the fish and vegetables. Discard the solids.

Store in the refrigerator for up to 3 days or freeze for longer.

## Vegetable Stock

| | | | | |
|---|---|---|---|---|
| 1 | tablespoon extra-virgin olive oil | | 1 | medium parsnip, scrubbed and halved |
| 2 | onions, roughly chopped | | 10 | peppercorns |
| | Salt | | 8 ½ | cups water |
| 2 | leeks, trimmed and roughly chopped | | 5 | sprigs fresh flat-leaf parsley, rinsed |
| 2 | carrots, scrubbed and roughly chopped | | 5 | sprigs fresh cilantro, rinsed |
| 2 | celery ribs, roughly chopped | | | |
| 2 | medium turnips, scrubbed and quartered | | | |

In a stockpot or another large, heavy pot, over medium heat, heat the oil. Add the onions and 2 generous pinches of salt and cook until soft and golden, about 5 minutes. Add the leeks, carrots, celery, turnips, and parsnip and cook, stirring occasionally, until they begin to release their juices, about 5 minutes. Add the peppercorns and cover with the water. Bring to a boil, reduce the heat, cover, and simmer for 1 hour.

Remove from the heat. Add the parsley and cilantro, push them down into the liquid, and let infuse as the stock cools.

Strain the broth through a fine mesh sieve, gently pressing out any remaining liquid from the vegetables. Discard the solids.

Store in the refrigerator for up to 3 or 4 days or freeze for longer.

# RICE RECIPES

# Mussel Dolmas / Midye dolması (Turkey)

At night, along Istanbul's main pedestrian thoroughfare, Istiklal Caddesi, and around the various terminals for ferries that crisscross the Bosphorus, hawkers lug out buckets of polished black mussels stuffed with rice, onions, currants, and pine nuts. They're perfect street food: split the bivalve, and you have your utensils—the empty part is the "plate," which cups the other (full) part, the "spoon." They're found in bars and boisterous *meyhanes*, too, washed down with glasses of *raki* (anise-flavored spirit). As the chef of the excellent meyhane Sanat told me, "Sixty to seventy percent of the taste is onion, ten to fifteen percent the spices, the rest mussels." A spritz of fresh lemon juice before eating gives a fresh tang. Broken grains of Baldo are ideal, giving off more starch and holding the stuffing tightly together.

| | |
|---|---|
| 24 | large mussels, trimmed and debearded |
| | Salt |
| 5 | tablespoons olive oil |
| 3 | medium onions, finely diced |
| 2 | tablespoons pine nuts |
| ½ | cup broken short- or medium-grain rice, preferably Baldo |
| | Freshly ground pepper |

| | |
|---|---|
| ⅛ | teaspoon ground cinnamon |
| ⅛ | teaspoon ground allspice |
| ⅛ | teaspoon ground cumin |
| ¼ | cup finely chopped fresh mint |
| 2 | tablespoons currants (see page 31) |
| | Juice of ½ lemon |
| 1 | cup water |
| 1 ½ | lemons, cut into about 12 wedges |

Soak the mussels in a bowl of warm salted water until they open slightly. Run the tip of a knife along the edge, prying open the shell; do not break the hinge. Rinse with fresh water and refrigerate until ready to stuff.

In a heavy sauté pan or skillet over low heat, heat the oil. Add the onions and pine nuts and cook, stirring from time to time, until sweet and translucent, 30 to 45 minutes.

Add the rice and cook for 5 minutes. Season with pepper and add the cinnamon, allspice, cumin, mint, currants, lemon juice, and ¹/₂ cup of the water. Cover, increase the heat to medium, and cook until the water is absorbed and the rice is about half cooked, around 8 minutes. Transfer to a bowl.

Stuff the mussels by placing a tablespoon of rice into each, closing the shell, and, if desired, securing it shut with a piece of cotton kitchen string. Place in a pot and pour in the remaining ¹/₂ cup of water. Place a plate over the mussels to hold down; keep covered and steam for 25 minutes or until the rice is cooked. Add a few more tablespoons of water to the pot, if needed, to avoid it drying out.

Transfer the mussels to a platter. Let cool to room temperature and refrigerate until serving.

Remove the string, if used, and wipe the mussels clean. Serve cold with the lemon wedges.

Cup the full side of the mussel shell in the empty one, squeeze some lemon juice over, and eat in a single bite.

# Tomato Dolmas with Ground Lamb, Rice, and Pine Nuts / Domates dolması (Turkey)

Broadly known as *dolma* in Turkey, *yemista* in Greece, and *mahshi* in Arabic, rice-stuffed vegetables can be divided into two categories: prepared with olive oil and served cold as part of a selection of appetizers, or prepared with meat mixed into the rice stuffing and served warm as part of a more substantial course. Serve this Turkish dolma with thick yogurt.

| | |
|---|---|
| 3 | tablespoons extra-virgin olive oil |
| 1 | medium onion, finely chopped |
| 2 | tablespoons pine nuts |
| ¼ | teaspoon ground allspice |
| ¼ | teaspoon ground cinnamon |
| | Salt and freshly ground pepper |
| ½ | cup short- or medium-grain rice, preferably Baldo |

| | |
|---|---|
| 2 | cups water |
| 8 | to 10 vine-ripened tomatoes |
| 8 | ounces ground lamb or veal (or a combination of both), preferably not too lean |
| 1 | heaping tablespoon finely chopped fresh flat-leaf parsley |
| 1 | teaspoon dried mint |
| 2 | cups thick natural yogurt |

In a heavy sauté pan or skillet over medium heat, heat the oil. Add the onion and pine nuts and cook until the onion is soft and translucent and the pine nuts are golden, about 10 minutes. Add the allspice, cinnamon, and salt and pepper, and then add the rice, stirring thoroughly to coat. Add 1 cup of the water and cook, uncovered, until all the water is absorbed and the rice is half cooked, about 9 minutes.

Meanwhile, using a sharp knife, cut off the caps from each tomato and reserve. With a small spoon, hollow out the tomatoes, being careful not to break the skin; discard the pulp. Generously season the insides of the tomatoes with salt and pepper.

Remove the rice from the heat and preheat the oven to 450°F.

In a medium bowl, mix together the rice, lamb, parsley, and mint into a smooth consistency.

Loosely stuff the tomatoes, replace the caps, and place the stuffed tomatoes in a roasting pan. Pour the remaining 1 cup of water around their bases, cover loosely with foil, and bake for 30 minutes or until the tomatoes are soft, the rice done, and the meat cooked.

Remove the foil, turn the oven to broil, and broil until the tops are browned, about 5 minutes. Remove from the oven and cover with the foil to keep warm until serving.

Serve with the yogurt on the side.

# Cabbage Rolls / Sarma (Croatia)

Of all the stuffed cabbage rolls I've eaten in Greece, Turkey, and the Balkans, the best by far were in Dubrovnik. Here, the leaves are soured, stuffed, and then long-simmered in a pot with a hefty piece of smoke-cured pancetta. (The woman who made the best-of-the-best rolls for me used her father's home-cured pancetta so deeply smoked it was black.) *Sarma* are best prepared the day before you wish to serve them and left in the pot overnight to soften and absorb the flavors. Place the rolls tightly in a pot; the tighter they are packed, the less water needed, which means a more flavorful sauce to spoon over top. Serve with mashed potatoes or polenta.

| | |
|---|---|
| 1 | head green cabbage, cored |
| 2 | tablespoons wine vinegar |
| 2 | bay leaves |
| | Salt and freshly ground pepper |
| 6 | ounces ground beef |
| 2 | ounces ground pork or fresh, unsweetened pork sausage pulled from the casing |
| 1 | medium onion, finely grated |

| | |
|---|---|
| ¼ | carrot, finely grated |
| 2 | garlic cloves, finely chopped |
| ⅓ | cup short- or medium-grain rice |
| 12 | ounces uncut smoked pancetta or bacon |
| 2 | tablespoons tomato concentrate, dissolved in ½ cup of warm water |
| 1 | teaspoon sweet pimentón (paprika) |
| 2 | tablespoons finely chopped fresh flat-leaf parsley |

In a large pot or stockpot, add the cabbage, vinegar, bay leaves, and some salt and pepper. Cover with water, bring to a boil, and let boil for 10 minutes. Remove the pot from the heat and let sit for 10 minutes. Carefully remove the cabbage and let cool. Gently separate the 12 best leaves.

In a large bowl, mix together the beef, pork, onion, carrot, garlic, and rice, seasoning with salt and pepper, to a smooth consistency.

Working with one leaf at a time, trim the fibrous raised center vein flush with the leaf. Place the leaf on a flat surface so that the edges naturally curl upward. Place about 2 tablespoons of filling along the widest part of the leaf. Fold the edges over and roll down to the open end, stretching and tucking the end around the roll. Repeat with the remaining 11 cabbage leaves and filling.

Chop any remaining cabbage and place it in the bottom of a large, heavy pot. Place the cabbage rolls against the edge of the pot in spoke formation, leaving a space in the center of the pot for the pancetta. Layer the rolls as needed. Cut the pancetta in half crosswise and place in the center gap. Add just enough water to cover the rolls. Mix the diluted tomato concentrate with the pimentón and pour the mixture into the pot. Place a bowl face-down on the top layer of rolls to keep them under the surface of the liquid. Bring to a simmer. Continue simmering for 2 hours over very low heat. Shake the pot from time to time but do not stir. Add more water, if needed, to keep the rolls covered.

Remove from the heat, cover, and let sit in the pot for at least 2 hours. Leave soaking until ready to serve.

To serve, gently reheat. Place the rolls in a shallow dish on the side and serve with the shredded cabbage and the pancetta, and spoon some juice over the top.

# Clams and Rice Served in the Shell (Dalmatia, Croatia)

Croatia's Dalmatian coast is known for its seafood and shellfish—the oysters of Ston are justifiably legendary—and its restaurants all serve variations of "shells salad." None that I ate, though, was as enticing as this one, which I have adapted from the locally published *Croatian Cookbook* by Nikica Gamulin Gama. Use different sizes and types of clams, cockles, even mussels and scallops; just be sure to have some large-sized ones to stuff. Serve as an appetizer with a bottle of chilled white wine or rosé on a warm day.

| | |
|---|---|
| 3 | pounds assorted clams, including some large-sized ones, purged of sand (see Note) |
| | Salt |
| ½ | cup short- or medium-grain rice |
| 8 | black olives, pitted and chopped |

| | |
|---|---|
| 8 | green olives, pitted and chopped |
| | Juice of 1 small lemon |
| 1 ½ | tablespoons extra-virgin olive oil |
| | Freshly ground pepper |

Fill a pot ¹/₂ to 1 inch deep with water and add the clams. Bring to a boil, cover, and steam until the clams have opened, about 5 minutes. Drain the clams and transfer to a platter to cool, discarding any that did not open.

Without breaking the hinges of the clams, remove the meat. Reserve the largest shells. Chop the meatier clams into pieces; leave the smaller ones whole.

Meanwhile, in another pot, bring an abundant amount of water to a boil, add a pinch of salt and the rice, and boil until al dente, 15 to 18 minutes. Drain the rice, rinse briefly under cold water, and drain again.

In a medium bowl, combine the rice with the clams and olives. Add the lemon juice, olive oil, and season with salt and pepper. Mix carefully.

Spoon the rice into the larger reserved shells and serve on a platter.

NOTE: TO PURGE CLAMS OF SAND, DISSOLVE 1 TEASPOON OF SALT IN 4 CUPS OF COOL WATER. ADD A FEW DROPS OF VINEGAR AND LET THE CLAMS SOAK FOR 30 MINUTES. CHANGE THE WATER, ADD MORE SALT, AND SOAK FOR ANOTHER 30 MINUTES. DRAIN, RINSE WELL WITH FRESH WATER, AND DRAIN AGAIN.

# Camargue Red Rice Salad with Shrimp / Salade camarguaise
## (Camarague, France)

In Piedmont, cooks stud summery, chilled long-grain rice salads with the garden's bounty. When I stayed at Tenuta Guazzaura, a three-hundred-year-old working farm with different grains and three varieties of grapes and a couple of guest apartments converted from old workers' quarters, the owners, Luca and his wife, Marie-Helen—the Counts Brondelli di Brondello—told me, "You are 99 percent sure it will be on the menu. It'll have vegetables, tomatoes, mozzarella, shrimp, beans, tomatoes, olive oil—never mayonnaise!"

Take away the mozzarella and perhaps the beans, and the same can be said about rice salads eaten in the Camargue, the Rhône River delta in southern Provence. Salads here often include locally grown red rice, giving the dish a delicious nuttiness and a stiffer, chewier body. Chervil, estragon, or other fresh herbs blend wonderfully into the vinaigrette.

|   |   |   |   |
|---|---|---|---|
|   | Salt | 3 | tablespoons red wine vinegar |
| 1 | cup Camargue red rice (see Note) | 1 | shallot, finely chopped |
| 1 | cup long-grain white rice |   | Freshly ground pepper |
| 4 | plum tomatoes, stemmed and chopped |   | French mustard |
| 2 | cucumbers, peeled and chopped | 24 | to 36 cooked jumbo shrimp or prawns, peeled |
| 36 | green olives | 3 | hard-boiled eggs, peeled and quartered lengthwise |
| ¾ | cup extra-virgin olive oil |   |   |

In a large pot, bring an abundant amount of water to a boil. Add 2 pinches of salt and the red rice and boil until al dente, 35 to 40 minutes. Drain the rice, rinse briefly under cold water, and drain again.

Meanwhile, in another pot, bring an abundant amount of water to a boil. Add a pinch of salt and the white rice and boil until al dente, 12 to 15 minutes. Drain the rice, rinse briefly under cold water, and drain again.

In a large bowl, combine the two rices with the tomatoes, cucumbers, and olives. Cover and refrigerate until ready to serve.

In a small bowl, add the oil and vinegar and whisk until cloudy. Add the shallots, season with salt and pepper, and whisk again until blended. Whisk in just enough of the mustard to taste.

When ready to serve, toss half of the vinaigrette with the rice. Divide the rice equally among six bowls, mounding the rice, and then place the shrimp and egg quarters on the rice. Drizzle the remaining vinaigrette over the top.

NOTE: THE RED RICE CAN BE SUBSTITUTED WITH AN EQUAL AMOUNT OF WHITE RICE, IN WHICH CASE THE SALAD WILL NEED SLIGHTLY LESS VINAIGRETTE.

**Primary Source: Robert Bon, Camargue, France**

At the mouth of the Rhône River, south of Arles, in the southwest tip of Provence, lies the wide Camargue delta, a remote place of bird-filled lagoons, checkerboards of drying salt pans that date back to antiquity, flamingos, semiwild white horses, and buff black bulls that are fought (and eaten!). The delta is also home to nearly all of the rice planted in France.

In the last days of summer, I drove leisurely among canal-fringed fields rippling with golden, ripening rice. A horse raised its head to watch me pass. A glistening white ibis lifted lethargically out of a swampy field; another perched on a hand-painted sign of a farmhouse that read RIZ in bold black letters.

Outside a village called La Sambuc, I turned down the long gravel drive of an old rice farm. A sign on the tall barn read:

J.BON et FILS
Rizerie du Petit Manusclat

The barn was now home to the Musée du Riz de Camargue. I was greeted by the *conservateur* (curator) of the museum, Robert Bon, a charismatic, middle-aged man with a large curling moustache, frayed straw hat, and quick laugh.

As we poked around the dusty displays of rice farming, he spoke at length about organic farming—a passionate topic: Robert's father, Joseph, was a pioneering organic rice farmer in the 1960s and the first to grow organic rice in Europe. We talked about short- and long-grain rice but also about *riz rouge*, an indigenous red rice crossed with short-grain japonica. Ruddy reddish-brown in color,

the rice has a pleasingly wildish taste and lovely toothy texture. "It goes with everything," he said. "Fish, vegetables, chicken, bull meat, ah yes, very nice . . ."

Known as Maître Robert Bon, for his *atelier du riz*, he also mans a stand in the vast Saturday street market in nearby Arles, an important Roman and medieval town on the eastern bank of the Rhône. "But where?" I asked. Miles of vendors from the lower Rhône valley sell everything from organic produce to fabric. "I'm by the carousel!"

On the way back home to Barcelona that next Saturday, my wife, girls, and I stopped in Arles and browsed through the market, buying olive oil, fresh goat cheese rolled in ash, a set of wood-handled Opinel table knives, and a traditional Provençal straw market basket (hand-woven in Madagascar). We eventually spotted the century-old wooden carousel and then Maître Bon. I wandered over to talk to him while my daughters bolted for the carousel.

Among the kilogram bags of different rices weighing down the table of his stand were small dishes filled with different types of rice grains. From a crockpot, he offered me a cup of red rice cooked with shallots, peppers, and tomatoes and seasoned with bay leaves and plenty of garlic.

A strong wind gusted, and he grabbed hold of the sun umbrella with one hand and his straw hat with the other, laughing as grains of rice scattered around the ancient square.

# Greek Chicken Soup with Egg and Lemon / Soupa avgolemono (Greece)

This creamy, chicken-studded version of Greece's best-known and most loved soup is as delicious as it is filling. The creaminess comes from puréeing the vegetables (not the chicken; that is hand shredded, otherwise it's unpleasantly gritty). A dollop of cold, thick yogurt is the perfect contrast to the warm smoothness of the soup and the zing of the egg-lemon sauce.

| | | | |
|---|---|---|---|
| 1 | whole chicken (about 3 ½ pounds) | 10 | cups water |
| | Salt and freshly ground pepper | ½ | cup short- or medium-grain rice |
| 1 | medium onion, peeled | 3 | large eggs, at room temperature |
| 1 | large or 2 small carrots, scrubbed | ½ | cup freshly squeezed lemon juice |
| 1 | stalk celery with leaves | ¼ | teaspoon oregano |
| 2 | bay leaves | 2 | cups thick natural yogurt |

Clean the chicken, discarding the giblets. Remove the skin and trim any excess fat. Rinse under running water and pat dry with paper towels. Cut into 4 or 6 pieces. Season generously with salt and pepper.

In a stockpot or another large pot, add the chicken, onion, carrot, celery, and bay leaves. Cover with the water, bring to a boil, and skim off any foam that comes up to the surface. Reduce the heat, partly cover, and simmer for 2 hours.

Transfer the chicken pieces with a slotted spoon to a platter to cool. Remove the vegetables and set aside. Strain the broth, discarding the herbs and any bones or other solids. Puree the vegetables and the broth in a food mill or blender. There should be 8 cups; blend in water as needed.

In a large, clean saucepan, bring the puréed broth to a boil. Add the rice, reduce the heat to low, cover, and cook until the rice is tender, about 20 minutes.

While the rice cooks, debone the chicken and shred the meat by hand into generous-sized pieces.

When the rice is cooked, remove the pot from the heat and add the shredded chicken. Taste for seasoning and adjust as needed.

In a bowl, whisk the eggs until foamy. Gradually work in the lemon juice and then, very slowly, 1 cup of the soup, stirring constantly. Slowly add the egg-lemon mixture into the soup along with the oregano while stirring constantly. If the soup needs to be reheated, do not allow it to boil (the eggs will curdle).

Serve in bowls with the yogurt on the side, letting everyone stir spoonfuls into their soup as desired.

## Lentils and Rice with Fried Onions / Mdardra (Lebanon)

This classic Lebanese dish has a dozen versions. Some eat it hot, and others like it at room temperature; it can be served a bit dry or quite moist. Its role, however, as pure homey comfort food is a constant. Here I offer the basic version. Stir in cumin or allspice to liven it up.

| | |
|---|---|
| 3 | large onions |
| 8 | tablespoons extra-virgin olive oil |
| 1 | heaping cup brown lentils, rinsed and drained |

| | |
|---|---|
| 5 | cups water |
| 1 | heaping cup short- or medium-grain rice |
| | Salt and freshly ground pepper |

Finely chop 1 of the onions. In a large, heavy pot over medium heat, heat 2 tablespoons of the oil. Add the chopped onion and cook until golden, about 10 minutes. Add the lentils and water, bring to a boil, reduce the heat, cover, and cook for 20 minutes. Add the rice, cover, and cook, stirring from time to time until the rice is tender and the liquid has been absorbed, about 20 minutes. Add more liquid if needed to keep it moist.

Meanwhile, cut the remaining 2 onions into thin slices. In a sauté pan or skillet, heat the remaining 6 tablespoons of oil. Add the onions and cook over low heat until they become soft and translucent, about 15 minutes. Increase the heat to high and cook until the onions are caramel brown, 7 to 10 minutes. Watch carefully that the onions do not burn, especially during the last few minutes. Remove with a slotted spoon and spread them onto a paper towel–lined plate to drain.

Taste the rice and lentils for seasoning and adjust as needed. Serve in bowls with the fried onions liberally scattered across the top.

# Sinarcas-Style Paella / Paella sinarqueña (Sinarcas, Valencia, Spain)

Both sides of my mother-in-law's family come from Sinarcas, a rural Valencian village where paella reigns supreme. Visiting means eating paella one day for lunch at Tía Encarnita's, another day at Tía Fermina's, the next at Tía Rosa's, and so on. And by paella there is just one kind: Valencian paella with rabbit, chicken, snails, and different types of fresh beans. This is Tía Encarnita's version (see page 51), which is started inside on the stove and then finished outside over a simmering fire of grape vines trimmed from the family vineyards.

Although snails are a key ingredient in Valencian paellas, they can be omitted. If you do use them, the smaller the snail the better; French escargot snails are simply too large for paella. Substitute *garrafons*—a variety of lima beans—with more green beans.

| | | | | |
|---|---|---|---|---|
| 2 | bone-in chicken thighs, skin and excess fat removed | | 12 | ounces green beans, ends trimmed and cut into 2-inch-long pieces |
| 2 | chicken legs, skin and excess fat trimmed | | 1 | tomato, peeled, seeded, and grated (see page 162) |
| ½ | rabbit (about 1 ½ pounds), fat trimmed and cut into 8 or so pieces | | 1 | tablespoon sweet pimentón (paprika) |
| | Salt | | 8 | ounces shucked fresh garrafons or lima beans |
| ½ | cup extra-virgin olive oil | | 20 | saffron threads, dry roasted and ground |
| 8 ½ | cups water | | 3 | cups Spanish short-grain Bomba rice |
| 24 | to 36 snails (see Note for preparation) | | | |

If the paella will be finished over fire or an outdoor grill, prepare the wood or embers.

Rinse the chicken and rabbit under running water. Pat dry with paper towels. Season generously with salt.

In a large sauté pan or skillet, heat the oil to smoking. Working in batches if necessary, fry the chicken and rabbit until deep golden brown, turning only occasionally, about 20 minutes total.

Meanwhile, begin the *caldo* (stock). Bring the water to a boil in a large pot. Add the prepared snails. Cover and keep at a low boil.

As the chicken and rabbit pieces become browned, transfer them to the caldo.

In the same oil, add the green beans and fry until slightly browned with some darker spots, about 5 minutes. Transfer with a slotted spoon to the caldo. Add the tomato to the same oil and fry for 2 minutes. Remove the pan from the heat, add the pimentón, and let cook, stirring frequently, for 2 minutes as the pan cools. Transfer the tomato and all of the oil to the caldo.

Cover and simmer the caldo for 10 minutes.

CONTINUED

Place an 18- to 20-inch paella pan on the stove top or outdoor grill. Pour in the caldo (there needs to be about 7 1/2 cups of liquid) and all of the meat and vegetables, bring to a boil, and boil for 5 minutes. Add the garrafons and saffron and let boil for another 5 minutes. Sprinkle in the rice and smooth it over with a wooden spoon to make sure the rice is evenly distributed and all of the grains are below the liquid's surface. Do not stir again. Cook, uncovered, for 10 minutes over high heat.

Reduce the heat to low (if using a gas grill, reduce the flame; wood and charcoal should be burned down to "low" by now) and cook for an additional 8 to 10 minutes until the liquid is absorbed and the rice has just a bite to it. If all the liquid has evaporated and the rice is not done, sprinkle tepid water tablespoon by tablespoon over the rice where needed and cook for a few additional minutes.

Remove the paella pan from the heat, cover with paper towels, and let rest for 5 minutes before serving. Place in the middle of the table and eat directly from the pan with spoons. Serve with toothpicks to extract the snail meat.

NOTE: TO PREPARE LIVE SNAILS, BEGIN BY SCRUBBING THE SHELLS CLEAN WITH PLENTY OF WATER AND A BIT OF VINEGAR. PLACE THE SNAILS IN A LARGE POT, COVER WITH ABUNDANT COLD WATER, AND BRING TO A BOIL. (NEVER ADD SNAILS TO BOILING WATER; THE GOAL IS TO KILL THEM SLOWLY SO THAT THE MEAT "HANGS" OUT AND DOESN'T RETRACT INTO THE SHELL.) BOIL FOR 1 HOUR. DRAIN, DISCARDING THE WATER, AND RINSE. TO PREPARE SNAILS PRESERVED IN BRINE, RINSE WELL AND THEN BOIL IN ABUNDANT WATER FOR 3 TO 4 MINUTES. DRAIN AND RINSE.

**Primary Source: Tía Encarnita, Sinarcas, Spain**

Sinarcas, a tiny, picturesque Spanish village surrounded by fields of grapes, wheat, and lavender, is an hour inland from Valencia. Both of my mother-in-law's parents are from here, and she spent her childhood shuttling between Sinarcas and Barcelona, where her father had a small *colmado* (grocery store) in the old city. There are still plenty of aunts and cousins in the village, and when my wife and two girls and I visit, we spend much of our time going (lurching!) from house to house, meal to meal. If it's lunch, we know we'll get paella.

In the summer, our first lunch in Sinarcas—and first paella!—is prepared by Tía Encarnita under the watchful eye of her sprightly, ninety-five-year-old mother, Tía Angelina.

As Tía Encarnita begins the paella in the kitchen, her husband, Nino, with a soggy, unlit stub of cigar clenched in his mouth, prepares the fire in the *corral*, an enclosed but open-air space that, until recently, used to be the domain of chickens as well as the spot where, each winter, a pig is butchered and preserved (mostly into different types of sausages). Now it's an extension of the large garage, with chords of vine trimmings stacked under a brick arch, ladders, an old tractor and moped, ropes, tools needed for looking after the family's vineyards, and a pair of lazy kittens. But one corner is reserved for Tía Encarnita's frequent paellas.

Once Nino lays the enormously wide pan on the iron fire stand and flames lick over its edges, Tía Encarnita transfers the cooked meats and stock to the pan, and then shakes in an entire kilogram of rice. Short and motherly, cheerful and loved by everyone, Tía Encarnita tends the paella with a practiced hand while chatting nonstop. Tía Angelina comes and goes, checking the paella, tasting it at one point, but saying little. She nods her wavy head of white hair and keeps her hands clasped together in front of her checkered apron.

Just as the rice is about done, my youngest daughter, Maia, wanders over and says perhaps the most distracting plea to any aunt or grandmother's ears: "I'm hungry!" As Tía Encarnita whisks her off to the kitchen for an immediate snack—even though lunch is moments away!—Tía Angelina shouts, "The paella is done! It'll burn! It needs to come off!"

As my mother-in-law is fond of saying: "Rice waits for no one!" Not even a precious three-year-old.

Nino slides carrying hooks into the handles and lifts the pan off the flames. After letting it rest for some minutes to firm up the starches, he carries it to the table. We dig right in, eating directly from the pan. The paella is perfect: tender, flavorful grains and a thin layer of slightly caramelized rice on the bottom called *socarrat*. The only noise was the scraping of ten spoons.

# Seafood Paella / Paella de marisco (Catalonia, Spain)

If Tía Encarnita's paella (see page 49) is a rural version of Spain's iconic dish, then this is an urban one, inspired by my mother-in-law's weekly seafood paella in Barcelona. While plenty of fresh cuttlefish gives a bounty of flavor, digging each grain of rice out of the clam shells gives the most pleasure. My daughters' incessant pleading for "*mes petxines*" (more shells) is a part of eating seafood paella with them.

| | | | | |
|---|---|---|---|---|
| 8 ½ | cups water | | 1 | red bell pepper, cored, seeded, and cut into 1-inch-square pieces |
| 8 | ounces small clams, purged of sand (see Note, page 43) | | 1 ½ | pounds cuttlefish or squid, cut into bite-sized pieces |
| | Salt | | 3 | tomatoes, peeled, seeded, and finely chopped |
| 8 | ounces mussels, scrubbed and debearded | | ½ | teaspoon sweet pimentón (paprika) |
| 6 | tablespoons extra-virgin olive oil | | 20 | saffron threads, dry roasted and ground |
| 18 | large or jumbo uncooked head-on shrimp with shells | | 2 ½ | cups Spanish short-grain Bomba rice |

In a large saucepan, bring 8 cups of the water to a boil. Add the clams and a pinch of salt, reduce the heat to low, partly cover, and simmer for 30 minutes. Remove from the heat, cover, and set aside.

Meanwhile, in a small saucepan over high heat, add the mussels and the remaining ½ cup of water. Bring to a boil, then lower the heat and simmer, uncovered, until all of the mussels have opened, 3 to 5 minutes. Discard any that did not open. Cover and keep in the pot until ready to use.

In a 16- to 18-inch paella pan over medium heat, heat the oil. Add the shrimp and cook until pink on each side, turning just once, about 2 minutes on each side. Transfer to a plate. Remove any solids left in the pan.

In the same oil, begin preparing a sofrito. In the center of the pan over medium heat, add the bell pepper and cook, stirring frequently, until it begins to brown and become fragrant, 3 to 5 minutes. Add the cuttlefish and cook until browned and its moisture has been expelled, stirring constantly and scraping anything that sticks to the pan, about 5 minutes. Add the tomatoes and season with salt and cook, gradually lowering the heat to low to avoid burning, until the tomatoes darken and lose their acidity, 10 to 12 minutes. Add a few tablespoons of water if the tomatoes look about to dry out.

Meanwhile, drain the clams, reserving the broth.

When the sofrito is ready, sprinkle in the pimentón and saffron, add the reserved clams and shrimp, and pour in 7 cups of the reserved clam liquid. Bring to a simmer. Continue to simmer for 10 minutes. Taste for seasoning and adjust as needed. Increase the heat, bring to a boil, sprinkle in the rice, and smooth it over with a

CONTINUED

wooden spoon to make sure the rice is evenly distributed and all of the grains are below the liquid's surface. Do not stir again. Cook, uncovered, for 10 minutes over high heat.

Reduce heat to low and cook for an additional 8 to 10 minutes until the liquid is absorbed and the rice has just a bite to it. If all the liquid has evaporated and the rice is not done, sprinkle tepid water tablespoon by tablespoon over the rice where needed and cook for an additional few minutes.

Meanwhile, remove and discard the empty half of each mussel shell.

Remove the paella pan from the heat, cover with paper towels, and let rest for 5 minutes. Poke the mussels into the rice, pointing wide lip up, around the pan. Serve immediately.

# Black Rice with Allioli / Arròs negre amb allioli (Costa Brava, Catalonia, Spain)

In many places along the European Mediterranean, flavoring and coloring rice and pasta with the ink of cuttlefish or squid is typical, from *crni rižoto* (black risotto) along Croatia's Dalmatian coast to spaghetti with squid ink in Sicily. This recipe comes from the Catalan Costa Brava, where *arròs negre* is a rustic fishermen's dish. Nothing is wasted of the cuttlefish here, even (or especially) the ink, with its intense distillation of the sea. Mixing pork or chicken with seafood is common in Catalonia, and here the pork ribs galvanize the flavors.

| | |
|---|---|
| 8 | ounces pork ribs, cut into ¾- to 1-inch-thick pieces |
| | Salt and freshly ground pepper |
| 3 | tablespoons extra-virgin olive oil |
| 1 | medium onion, finely chopped |
| ½ | green bell pepper, cored, seeded, and cut into 1-inch-square pieces |
| 2 | garlic cloves, finely chopped |
| 1 | pound cuttlefish or squid, cleaned, cut into 1-inch-square pieces, the ink sacks reserved (see Note) |

| | |
|---|---|
| 3 | tomatoes, peeled, seeded, and finely chopped |
| 6 | cups Fish Stock (page 34) |
| 6 | toasted almonds, skins slipped off |
| 1 | tablespoon finely chopped fresh flat-leaf parsley |
| 1 | teaspoon sweet pimentón (paprika) |
| 25 | saffron threads, dry roasted and ground |
| 2 | cups Spanish short-grain Bomba rice |
| | Allioli (page 57) |

Generously season the pork ribs with salt and pepper.

In a cazuela, Dutch oven, or another large, heavy pot over medium heat, heat the oil. Add the pork ribs and cook, stirring frequently, until they take on a bit of color, about 5 minutes. Add the onion and cook until it begins to soften, about 5 minutes. Add the green bell pepper and 1 of the garlic cloves, and cook, stirring frequently, for another 5 minutes. Add the cuttlefish and cook for 5 minutes and then add the tomatoes. Cook, continuing to stir frequently, until the tomato darkens and loses its acidity, 10 to 15 minutes. Add a few tablespoons of stock if the mixture looks about to dry out.

Meanwhile, make the picada. In a mortar, pound the remaining garlic clove, almonds, and parsley with a pestle into a gritty paste, loosened with 1 or 2 tablespoons of stock, as necessary; or quickly blend them in a food processor with 1 or 2 tablespoons of stock. Set aside.

Sprinkle the pimentón and saffron into the pan and then pour in the remaining stock. Increase the heat to medium-high heat and bring to a boil. Stir in the ink and add the rice. Cook, uncovered, for 10 minutes. Stir in the picada. Taste for seasoning and adjust as needed. Reduce the heat to low and cook for another 7 to 8 minutes or just until the rice has a bite to it.

Remove the cazuela from the heat and immediately transfer the rice to plates. Let the rice rest a few minutes before serving with the allioli.

NOTE: MERCURY COLORED INK SACKS ARE FOUND BENEATH THE TENTACLES OF CUTTLEFISH AND SQUID; REMOVE THEM CAREFULLY WHEN CLEANING (OR ASK YOUR FISHMONGER TO RESERVE THEM IF PURCHASING IT CLEANED). CERTAIN ASIAN AND ITALIAN MARKETS SELL PACKETS OF PRESERVED SQUID INK; TWO 4-GRAM ($^1/_2$-OUNCE) PACKETS ARE ENOUGH FOR THIS RECIPE.

## Allioli

This classic garlicky sauce is found across Valencia and Catalonia, and in Provence where it's called *aïoli*. The traditional Catalan version is laboriously pounded in a mortar with its two namesake ingredients, garlic (*all*) and (*i*) olive oil (*oli*). This quicker, much simpler version uses an egg as a binder and is blended with an immersion hand blender (called *batedora de brazo* or *minipiner* in Spain) or food processor.

| | | | | |
|---|---|---|---|---|
| 1 | large garlic clove, peeled | | 6 | tablespoons sunflower oil |
| 1 | large egg, at room temperature | | ⅛ | teaspoon salt |
| 6 | tablespoons olive oil | | ⅛ | teaspoon white pepper |

If using a hand blender: In a tall, narrow container just slightly larger than the diameter of the hand blender's shaft, add the garlic, then the egg, olive and sunflower oils, salt, and white pepper. With the hand blender off, place the shaft in the bottom of the container. Begin blending at three-fourths speed. When an emulsion begins to form, slowly move the hand blender up until the blade is just above the surface, back down, and then back up and out; total blending time is about 45 seconds. The allioli should have the consistency of mayonnaise; creamy but with no pooled oil.

If using a food processor: Add the garlic, egg, olive and sunflower oils, salt, and white pepper. Using short pulses, blend until the allioli has the consistency of mayonnaise; creamy but with no pooled oil.

Spoon the allioli into a small serving dish, tightly cover with plastic wrap, and refrigerate until ready to serve. Just before serving, rewhisk with a spoon. Tightly covered, it can be stored in the refrigerator for up to 2 days.

# Rice with Monkfish and Artichokes /
# Arròs amb rap i carxofes (Ebro Delta, Spain)

One of the keys to this rich, moist Catalan rice dish is the picada (see page 28). Pounded almonds, hazelnuts, garlic, and parsley change the flavor and color of the rice and thicken the consistency. Keep the picada firmly in the background by pounding the nuts fine enough so that no recognizable pieces can be found in the rice.

| | |
|---|---|
| 3 | cups water |
| 6 | ounces small clams, purged of sand (see Note, page 43) |
| | Salt |
| 1 | pound monkfish, cut into 8 steaks |
| | Freshly ground pepper |
| 3 | tablespoons extra-virgin olive oil |
| 1 | medium onion, finely chopped |
| 4 | medium artichokes, trimmed, tough parts of the leaves removed, cut into eighths, and choke scraped out |

| | |
|---|---|
| 7 ½ | cups Fish Stock (page 34) |
| 1 | garlic clove, peeled |
| 6 | toasted almonds, skins slipped off |
| 6 | toasted hazelnuts, skins slipped off |
| 1 | heaping teaspoon finely chopped fresh flat-leaf parsley |
| 1 | teaspoon sweet pimentón (paprika) |
| 20 | saffron threads, dry roasted and ground |
| 2 | cups Spanish short-grain Bomba rice |

In a medium saucepan, bring the water to a boil. Add the clams and a pinch of salt, reduce the heat to low, partly cover, and simmer until the clams have opened, less than 5 minutes. Remove from the heat, cover, and set aside.

Season the monkfish generously with salt and pepper. In a cazuela, Dutch oven, or another large, heavy pot over medium heat, heat the oil. Add the fish and fry, turning just once, until golden, 1 to 2 minutes per side. Transfer to a platter.

In the same oil, add the onion and cook, stirring frequently, until soft and nearly translucent, 5 to 10 minutes. Add the artichokes and cook for another 5 minutes. Ladle in 1 cup of the fish stock and simmer until evaporated, about 10 minutes.

Meanwhile, drain the clams, reserving the broth. Discard any clams that did not open.

Prepare the picada. In a mortar, pound the garlic, almonds, hazelnuts, and parsley with a pestle into a gritty paste, loosened with 1 or 2 tablespoons of the reserved clam broth, as necessary; or quickly blend them in a food processor with 1 or 2 tablespoons of the reserved clam broth. Set aside.

Once the stock has evaporated, sprinkle the pimentón and saffron into the cazuela and then pour in the remaining 6½ cups of fish stock. Increase the heat, bring to a boil, and add the rice and clams. Cook, uncovered, over medium-high heat for 10 minutes, gently stirring from time to time. Spoon in the picada. Taste for seasoning and adjust as needed. Lay the monkfish steaks across the top of the rice, reduce the heat to low, and cook until most of the liquid is absorbed and the rice has just a bite to it, about 8 minutes. The rice should be moist; add a little reserved clam broth if needed.

Remove the cazuela from the heat and immediately transfer the rice to plates. Let the rice rest for a few minutes before serving.

# Soupy Rice of Clams, Shrimp, and Wild Mushrooms / Arroz caldoso de almejas, gambas y setas (Spain)

The picada in this coastal Spanish dish includes *ñora* peppers—small, round, dried sweet red peppers that bring an added robustness of flavor. Ñoras are soaked in water to soften, lightly fried in oil, and then pounded with the picada. If you cannot find ñora peppers, use an ancho chile or 1 tablespoon of sweet pimentón dissolved in just enough water to form a paste.

| | |
|---|---|
| 2 | small ñora peppers |
| 3 | cups water |
| 12 | ounces clams, purged of sand (see Note, page 43) |
| | Salt |
| 5 | tablespoons extra-virgin olive oil |
| 1 | garlic clove, minced |
| 1 | small slice day-old country bread |
| 1 | teaspoon finely chopped fresh flat-leaf parsley |
| 8 | whole toasted almonds, skins slipped off |

| | |
|---|---|
| 10 | cups Fish Stock (page 34) |
| 12 | ounces large uncooked head-on shrimp with shells |
| 1 | leek (white and tender green parts only), finely chopped |
| 12 | ounces mixed wild mushrooms (see Note) |
| ½ | teaspoon sweet pimentón (paprika) |
| 20 | saffron threads, dry roasted and ground |
| 2 | cups Spanish short-grain Bomba rice |
| | Freshly ground pepper |

Soak the ñora peppers in a small bowl of warm water for 1 hour; drain. Remove and discard the stems and seeds; then chop and set aside.

In a large saucepan, bring the 3 cups water to a boil. Add the clams and a pinch of salt, reduce the heat to low, partly cover, and simmer until the clams have opened, less than 5 minutes. Remove from the heat, cover, and set aside.

Meanwhile, prepare the picada. In a small sauté pan or skillet over medium-low heat, heat 1 tablespoon of the oil. Cook the ñora peppers and the garlic over medium-low heat until the garlic is golden, about 5 minutes, watching carefully that it does not burn. Transfer the mixture to a mortar. Using a pestle, pound the pepper and garlic mixture with the bread, parsley, and almonds into a fine paste, loosened with 1 or 2 tablespoons of stock, as necessary; or quickly blend them in a food processor with 1 or 2 tablespoons of stock.

In a tall cazuela, Dutch oven, or another large, heavy pot over medium heat, heat 3 tablespoons of the oil. Add the shrimp and cook until they change color, turning only once. Transfer to a platter and decrease the heat to medium low. In the same oil, add the leek and cook until soft and translucent, 5 to 10 minutes.

Meanwhile, in a sauté pan or skillet over high heat, heat the remaining 1 tablespoon of oil. Add the mushrooms and cook until slightly caramelized, about 5 minutes. Remove from the heat, cover, and set aside.

CONTINUED

Drain the clams, reserving the broth. Discard any clams that did not open.

When the leeks are soft, sprinkle in the pimentón and saffron, and then pour in the stock. Increase the heat, bring to a boil, and add the rice and clams. Cook, uncovered, over medium-high heat for 10 minutes, gently stirring from time to time. Spoon in the picada, add the shrimp and mushrooms (and any juices in the pan), and cook for an additional 8 minutes, or until the rice has just a bite to it. Taste for seasoning and adjust as needed. Add a little reserved clam broth to make it soupier if desired.

Remove the rice from the heat, cover with a lid, and bring to the table. Lift the lid, allowing the aromas to waft out. Ladle into bowls immediately.

NOTE: LET THE SEASON DICTATE THE CHOICE OF MUSHROOMS, FROM MORELS IN SPRING TO CHANTERELLES IN AUTUMN. AS A GENERAL RULE, MUSHROOMS FOUND WILD IN THE WOODS SHOULD BE BRUSHED CLEAN; THOSE BOUGHT IN MARKETS SHOULD BE QUICKLY DUNKED IN A FEW CHANGES OF COOL WATER JUST BEFORE COOKING.

## Asparagus Risotto / Risotto agli asparagi (Northern Italy)

The first true, and truly good, risotto I ever ate was a spring one with asparagus and herbs cut fresh from the garden. The asparagus had been blanched just for a moment and retained a crunch that contrasted wonderfully with the creaminess of the rice. And though I've eaten plenty of variations of risotto since, this remains a favorite. At home we sometimes toss in a handful of freshly shucked peas or maybe, as a treat (and if I've been to La Boqueria market that day), some fresh morels. Fresh herbs, like thyme, basil, tarragon, and even mint, harmonize with other flavors with ease. But at this dish's center is always the slightly crunchy asparagus. This is the basic version; add to it at will, just as we do.

|   |   |
|---|---|
|   | Salt |
| 12 | ounces fresh asparagus, thick ends snapped off and discarded |
| 8 | cups Chicken Stock (page 33) or Vegetable Stock (page 35) |
| 1 | cup dry white wine |
| 3 | tablespoons extra-virgin olive oil |

|   |   |
|---|---|
| 1 | small onion, finely chopped |
| 1 ¾ | cups Carnaroli rice |
| 2 | tablespoons butter, cut into small pieces |
| 1 ½ | ounces freshly grated Parmigiano-Reggiano |
|   | Freshly ground pepper |

Fill a large basin with ice water. In a large pot, bring an abundant amount of water to a rolling boil, add 2 generous pinches of salt, and blanch the asparagus by dunking them into boiling water for 2 minutes and then immediately plunging them into the basin of cold water to stop any further cooking. Once they have cooled, remove with a slotted spoon and drain. Snap off the soft tips and set aside. Chop the remaining asparagus into ¹/₂- to 1-inch-long pieces. (The thicker the asparagus, the shorter the pieces.) Set aside separate from the tips.

In a large saucepan, bring the stock to a simmer, reduce the heat, and keep hot. Gently warm the wine.

In a deep, heavy saucepan over medium heat, heat the oil. Add the onion and a healthy pinch of salt and cook until the onion is soft and translucent but not yet browned, 8 to 10 minutes. Add the rice, stir well, and cook until slightly toasted, 3 to 4 minutes.

Add the wine and cook, stirring continually as it sizzles and jumps, scraping anything that has stuck to the pan, until the liquid has evaporated, less than 1 minute. Begin adding the stock a ladleful at a time, stirring only after adding liquid. Once the stock is absorbed, add the next ladleful. Continue adding until the rice is just about al dente, 20 to 30 minutes. There may be a small amount of stock left over; if you run out, use hot water.

Remove the pan from the heat and stir in a generous final ladleful of stock. Add the butter and half of the cheese and stir lightly to blend into the rice. Grind some pepper over top. Stir in the cut segments of asparagus (not the tips). Taste for seasoning and adjust with salt and pepper as needed. The rice should be moist and creamy, with a slight ripple across its surface when the pan is stiffly shaken. Stir in another ladleful of stock if needed.

Spread the asparagus tips evenly across the top of the rice. Let the rice rest for 2 minutes and serve in warm bowls with the remaining cheese on the side.

# The Countess's Whiskey Risotto with Rosemary /
# Risotto con rosmarino (Vercelli, Italy)

Countess Rosetta Clara Cavalli d'Olivola, with her son Paolo, owns and runs Principato di Lucedio, Italy's finest rice producer (see page 66). She passed me this recipe when we were together on her farm outside Vercelli, and it instantly became a dinner staple back home. About a year later in Barcelona, over a hearty, late breakfast of head and foot stew (and glasses of cava) inside La Boqueria market, the countess casually mentioned that she prefers to add not the standard white wine to her rosemary risotto as she had previously said, but rather whiskey. That night I trimmed some rosemary from the shrub on my terrace and rummaged in my drink cabinet for a forgotten bottle of whiskey. The changes were distinct. The clean and tangy notes of the wine were replaced with earthy and rustic ones—an even better match for the rosemary.

| | |
|---|---|
| 8 | cups Chicken Stock (page 33) or Vegetable Stock (page 35) |
| ½ | cup whiskey or 1 cup dry white wine |
| 3 | tablespoons extra-virgin olive oil |
| 4 | sprigs of rosemary, leaves only, finely chopped (about 2 tablespoons) |

| | |
|---|---|
| 1 ¾ | cups Carnaroli rice |
| | Salt and freshly ground pepper |
| 2 | tablespoons butter, cut into small pieces |
| 2 | ounces freshly grated Parmigiano-Reggiano |

In a saucepan, bring the stock to a simmer, reduce the heat, and keep hot. Gently warm the whiskey.

In a deep, heavy saucepan over medium heat, heat the oil. Add the rosemary and gently fry for 1 to 2 minutes, making sure it doesn't burn.

Add the rice, stir well, and cook until slightly toasted, 3 to 4 minutes. Add a pinch of salt and pepper.

Add the whiskey and cook, stirring continually as it sizzles and jumps, scraping anything that has stuck to the pan, until the liquid has evaporated, less than 1 minute. Begin adding the stock a ladleful at a time, stirring only after adding liquid. Once the stock is absorbed, add the next ladleful. Continue adding until the rice is just about al dente, 20 to 30 minutes. There may be a small amount of stock left over; if you run out, use hot water.

Remove the pan from the heat and stir in a generous final ladleful of stock. Add the butter and half of the cheese and stir lightly to blend into the rice. Taste for seasoning and adjust as needed. The rice should be moist and creamy, with a slight ripple across its surface when the pan is stiffly shaken. Stir in another ladleful of stock if needed.

Let the rice rest for 2 minutes and serve in warm bowls with the remaining cheese on the side.

### Primary Source: Countess Rosetta Clara Cavalli d'Olivola, Po River Valley, Northern Italy

Italy produces the bulk of its rice on the plains of the Po River Valley, between Milan and Turin and just north of the Piedmontese mountains. The rice fields are flooded in spring, creating a gorgeous mirrored checkerboard among farmsteads, poplar trees, and frog-rich canals. Vibrant greens gradually fill in as the rice steadily grows until autumn when—the stalks heavy with golden grains of rice—it's harvested.

During a recent harvest, I joined Countess Rosetta Clara Cavalli d'Olivola. She owns and manages Principato di Lucedio, Italy's oldest, and finest, rice farm. Documents show that the first rice cultivated in northern Italy was on this very farm, around 1400.

The countess is generous and charming, short and skinny, and has a lively sense of humor. She was born in Turin and spent summers on the farm as a girl, before moving here full time when she took it over. As we walked around the outbuildings for milling and packaging, splendid dining halls, and the ancient Abbey of Lucedio founded by Cistercian monks in A.D. 1123, she talked at length about risotto, not just what rice to use ("Carnaroli!") or how often to stir ("Only when you add stock!"), but about the culture of rice farming.

We stopped at a row of brick buildings that once housed seasonal workers. "In 1957 there were five-hundred rice weeders in spring and four-hundred cutters in autumn on the farm," she explained. "They ate only rice. They brought with them a cook from Veneto, who was paid in rice." She shook her head. "Now there are just two machines, fourteen tractors, and five people working in the fields plus another three in the office. Eight total!"

If rice farming has changed, then so have risottos. "There were only four kinds of risotto when I was growing up: with mushrooms, *alla milanese* [with saffron], with Parmigiano-Reggiano, and, in autumn, with truffles," she laughed. "Now risottos are eaten with every vegetable, even with strawberries and the juices of pomegranates. My uncle wouldn't touch these!" She laughed again. "But I make a wonderful strawberry risotto. With calvados!"

# Risotto with Porcini Mushrooms and Scallops /
# Risotto con porcini e capasante (Northern Italy)

Not far from the Principato di Lucedio rice farm, in the tiny village of Livorno Ferraris, is Silvestro Angelo's rustic Ristorante Balin. Silvestro is a funny, big-hearted, and talented chef whose superb country-style risottos draw people from the region's cities. Lunch there one autumn day consisted of five courses of rice, including two risottos, the most impressive brought out inside a great wheel of local Grana Padano. Silvestro mixed the rice, gently scraping away at the cheese, and then ladled the very creamy risotto onto the plate. This risotto, adapted from one of Angelo's recipes, is more elegant and, for me, even more delicious.

| | | | | |
|---|---|---|---|---|
| 6 | cups Vegetable Stock (page 35) | | | Salt and freshly ground pepper |
| 1 | cup dry white wine | | 1 ½ | tablespoons butter |
| 4 | tablespoons extra-virgin olive oil | | 4 | ounces fresh scallops (8 to 16, depending on size) |
| 1 ½ | cups Carnaroli rice | | ½ | tablespoon chopped fresh celery leaves |
| ½ | tablespoon minced garlic | | ½ | tablespoon chopped fresh thyme |
| ½ | tablespoon minced scallions | | | |
| 8 | ounces cleaned fresh porcini mushrooms, sliced lengthwise into flat silhouettes | | | |

In a saucepan, bring the stock to a simmer, reduce the heat, and keep hot. Gently warm the wine.

In a deep, heavy saucepan over medium heat, heat the oil. Add the rice, stir well, and cook until slightly toasted, 3 to 4 minutes. Add the garlic, scallions, and two-thirds of the mushrooms. Season with salt and pepper and cook, stirring continually, for 1 minute until the garlic begins to become fragrant.

Add the wine and cook, stirring continually as it sizzles and jumps, scraping anything that has stuck to the pan, until the liquid has evaporated, less than 1 minute. Begin adding the stock a ladleful at a time, stirring only after adding liquid. Once the stock is absorbed, add the next ladleful. Continue adding until the rice is just about

al dente, 20 to 30 minutes. There may be a small amount of stock left over; if you run out, use hot water.

Meanwhile, in a small sauté pan or skillet over medium heat, melt the butter. Add the scallops and cook until they have a light brown crust, turning just once, 4 to 5 minutes on each side. Transfer to a dish and cover to keep warm.

In the same butter, add the remaining one-third of the mushrooms. Cook until browned, about 2 minutes, add a few tablespoons of stock, scalding them with the steam, for 1 minute to slightly soften. Sprinkle with half of the celery and thyme and then return the scallops to the pan, laying them on top to absorb the flavor of the herbs. Remove the pan from the heat and cover to keep warm.

CONTINUED

When the rice is done, remove the pan from the heat and stir in a generous final ladleful of stock. Add the remaining celery and thyme and stir lightly just until blended. Taste for seasoning and adjust as needed. The rice should be moist and creamy, with a slight ripple across its surface when the pan is stiffly shaken. Stir in another ladleful of stock if needed.

Let rest for 2 minutes. Divide among warm bowls and top with the mushrooms and scallops.

# Venetian Rice with Fresh Peas / Risi e bisi (Venice, Italy)

Venetians once devoured *risi e bisi*—literally "rice and peas"—to celebrate the city's patron saint San Marco (Saint Mark) on April 25, when tender baby peas fill the markets. Now it's a popular dish enjoyed far more often, with good reason.

Short, stocky Vialone Nano rice is perfect here, but any other good risotto rice will work. The final consistency is runnier than a risotto; runny enough to need a spoon to fully enjoy it. The surface of the rice should be *all'onda* (wavy) when the pan is stiffly shaken.

| | | | | |
|---|---|---|---|---|
| 2 | pounds fresh peas in the pod (see Note) | | 3 | ounces lean pancetta, chopped |
| 8 ½ | cups water | | 1 ⅓ | cups Vialone Nano rice |
| | Salt | | | Freshly ground pepper |
| 3 | tablespoons butter | | 2 | tablespoons finely chopped fresh flat-leaf parsley |
| 1 | medium onion, finely chopped | | 2 | ounces freshly grated Parmigiano-Reggiano |

Shuck the peas into a bowl of fresh, cool water to keep moist, reserving the pods. Rinse the pods under running water.

Bring 8 ½ cups of water to a boil, add 2 pinches of salt, and then add the pods. Reduce the heat and simmer uncovered for 1 hour. Strain the stock through a sieve, discarding the solids. There should be at least 6 cups of sweet, fragrant broth; add water to make up any difference. Transfer the broth to a clean saucepan and keep hot.

In a deep, heavy saucepan over medium-low heat, melt the butter. Add the onion and pancetta and cook until the onion softens and is translucent, about 10 minutes. Add the rice, stir well, and cook until slightly toasted, 3 to 4 minutes. Add 6 cups of the hot, reserved broth.

Drain and add the peas. Season with salt and pepper. Bring to a simmer. Continue simmering gently until the rice is al dente, 15 to 17 minutes. The final consistency needs to be runny; add more broth as needed.

Remove the pan from the heat. Stir in the parsley and the cheese. Taste for seasoning and adjust as needed. A stiff shake of the pan should cause waves on the surface. Stir in another ladleful of broth (or hot water) if needed. Serve in warm bowls with spoons.

NOTE: FRESHLY SHUCKED ENGLISH OR GARDEN PEAS REQUIRE 12 TO 15 MINUTES OF COOKING. BABY PEAS, SOMETIMES CALLED *PETITS POIS*, NEED VERY LITTLE COOKING TIME AND CAN BE ADDED JUST BEFORE THE RICE IS DONE.

# Pilaf with Eggplant / Patlıcanlı pilav (Turkey)

Eggplant is Turkey's favorite vegetable, and the sheer number of different ways that it's prepared offers a perfect example of the ingenuity and diversity of the country's cuisine. Among the dozens of different preparations, fried and scattered over pilaf is a firm favorite. Cutting and salting the eggplant before cooking draws out some of the bitter liquid. Be sure to wash the pieces very well before frying to avoid excessive saltiness in the dish. Fry in batches to avoid crowding the pan and reducing the heat of the oil, which leads to soggy, oil-laden pieces of eggplant.

| | | | |
|---|---|---|---|
| 1 | large or 2 small eggplant (about 1 pound) | ¼ | teaspoon ground cinnamon |
| | Salt | | Freshly ground pepper |
| 1 ½ | cups long-grain rice | 2 ½ | cups water |
| ¼ | cup extra-virgin olive oil | | Sunflower oil for frying |
| 1 ½ | medium onions, finely chopped | 2 | tablespoons butter |
| ¼ | teaspoon ground allspice | 2 | heaping tablespoons pine nuts |

Wash the eggplant and cut into 1-inch-square cubes. Liberally salt and place in a colander to drain for 30 minutes. Rinse thoroughly with cool running water and gently squeeze out some of the excess liquid. Pat dry with paper towels.

Rinse the rice with a number of changes of cool water until the water runs clear. Place in a bowl, add 1 tablespoon of salt, and cover with warm water. Stir and allow to cool. Drain, rinse, and drain again.

In a large, heavy saucepan or pot over medium heat, heat the olive oil. Add the onions and cook until soft and translucent, about 10 minutes. Stir in the allspice and cinnamon and season with salt and pepper. Add the rice and stir to coat. Add the 2 $^1/_2$ cups water and bring to a boil. Stir, cover with a tight-fitting lid, and cook over low heat without stirring or lifting the lid for 7 minutes. With a wide, round spatula, turn the rice over to ensure even cooking. Immediately replace the lid and cook until the rice absorbs the liquid and is done but still firm, another 5 to 7 minutes depending on the rice; check after

5 minutes. If the rice is too moist, remove the lid; if it's too dry, sprinkle in some warm water. Remove from the heat.

Meanwhile fry the eggplant. In a large sauté pan or skillet over high heat, heat about 1 inch deep of the sunflower oil to smoking. Working in batches, fry the pieces until golden on the outside and tender on the inside when poked with the tip of a sharp knife. Remove with a slotted spoon and lay on a paper towel–lined plate to drain.

In a small saucepan over medium-low heat, melt the butter. Add the pine nuts and cook, stirring frequently, until golden, about 5 minutes.

Remove the lid from the rice and gently fold in the eggplant and pine nuts with any remaining melted butter. Place a clean kitchen towel over the pot and replace the lid snuggly. Let sit in a warm corner of the kitchen for 40 minutes to 1 hour before serving.

With a large serving spoon, gently transfer the rice to a serving dish, taking care not to mash or break the rice.

# Tomato Pilaf / Domatesli pilav (Turkey)

On a recent hot summer day in Istanbul, walking around the 19th-century backstreets of Beyoğlu, I ducked into a small side-street eatery. Chalked up on the board were the day's specials: *ayran aşi*— a slightly tart cold yogurt soup with bulgur and chickpeas—and *domatesli pilav*—a simple pilaf made with ripe, flavorful tomatoes. A perfect summer lunch.

| | | | | |
|---|---|---|---|---|
| 1 ½ | cups long-grain rice | | 1 | tablespoon sugar |
| | Salt | | 2 ½ | cups water |
| 4 | tablespoons extra-virgin olive oil | | | Freshly ground pepper |
| 3 | tomatoes, halved, seeded, and grated (see page 162) | | | |

Rinse the rice with a number of changes of cool water until the water runs clear. Place in a bowl, add 1 tablespoon of salt, and cover with warm water. Stir and allow to cool. Drain, rinse, and drain again.

In a large, heavy saucepan or pot over medium heat, heat the oil. Add the tomatoes and cook, stirring frequently, until they begin to soften and lose their acidity, about 15 minutes. Reduce the heat to low toward the end. Add in a small amount of water if the tomatoes look about to dry out.

Stir in the rice and sugar, season with salt, and stir to coat. Add the 2½ cups water and bring to a boil. Stir, cover with a tight-fitting lid, and cook over low heat without stirring or lifting the lid for 7 minutes. With a wide, round spatula, turn the rice over to ensure even cooking. Immediately replace the lid, and cook until the rice absorbs the liquid and is done but still firm, another 5 to 7 minutes depending on the rice; check after 5 minutes. If the rice is too moist, remove the lid; if it's too dry, sprinkle in some warm water. Remove from the heat.

Remove the lid from the rice, place a clean kitchen towel over the pot, and replace the lid snuggly. Let sit in a warm corner of the kitchen for 40 minutes to 1 hour before serving.

With a large serving spoon, gently transfer the rice to a serving dish, taking care not to mash or break the rice. Grind pepper over the top and serve.

**Primary Source: Ergin Sönmezler, Yanyalı, Istanbul**

One warm August Sunday, I took the ferry across the Bosphorus from the European side of Istanbul to Kadiköy on the Asian side, where the strait opens wide-mouthed into the Sea of Marmara. The scenic crossing takes twenty minutes; just long enough to enjoy a *simit* (bread ring) covered in sesame seeds and a tulip-shaped glass of *çay* (black tea), two simple pleasures that always evoke my first trips to Istanbul a dozen years ago.

In Kadıköy, I browsed the small streets behind the old Mustafa Iskele Mosque: fishmongers, spice shops (to buy sumac, mastic, and black cumin seeds), yogurt and cheese shops, greengrocers, bakeries (including my favorite, Eser Ekmet, across from the Armenian church), and dozens of used bookshops. I'd come, though, to eat lunch at Yanyalı, perhaps the city's best *lokanta* (a basic restaurant where the day's dishes are laid out to choose from), and spend some more time with the friendly, thirty-something Ergin Sönmezler.

In 1919, at the very end of the Ottoman Empire, Ergin's grandfather, Fehmi Sönmezler, decided to open a restaurant and approached one of the palace chefs to lead the kitchen. Nearly ninety years later, the same traditional dishes are being prepared with the same exacting standards of quality and freshness. The extensive, rotating menu exhibits the breadth and wealth of traditional Turkish cuisine.

As good as every one of the dozens of dishes looked, I came specifically to sample, under Ergin's guidance, Yanyalı's array of rice dishes.

I began with various stuffed vegetable dolmas—cold ones with rice, pine nuts, and currants, as well as warm ones with rice and meat—and then moved on to the pilafs. I ate glistening white plain pilaf made with chestnut oil, a salmon-colored tomato pilaf, eggplant pilaf garnished with fresh dill, and a superb *iç pilav* studded with pieces of lamb liver, tiny currants, and pine nuts and delicately seasoned with black pepper, allspice, and a pinch of cinnamon. In each, the grains of rice were individual and fluffy and glistened with oil and butter. Perfect.

"What's the trick?" I asked Ergin.

"There is no trick," he said. "It's technique."

Pilaf was an exam dish for Ottoman palace chefs. Still a gauge of quality, it's how you can tell a good restaurant: if the pilaf is good, the restaurant is good. (And the pilaf at Yanyalı was very good.)

Two desserts at Yanyalı—*fırın sütlaç*, a creamy baked rice pudding, and *zerde*, a translucent saffron-colored rice-flour pudding—left absolutely no room for a beloved *simit* on the ferry ride back. But another glass of *çay*? Always.

# Pilaf with Liver, Pistachios, Pine Nuts, and Currants / Iç pilav (Turkey)

*Iç pilav* is a much-loved Turkish dish, served at feasts and festivals, at weddings and funerals. The combination of ingredients is nearly perfect. This recipe uses lamb liver, although it can be also made with chicken livers.

| | | | | |
|---|---|---|---|---|
| 1 ½ | cups long-grain rice | | 3 | tablespoons butter |
| | Salt | | 4 | ounces lamb or chicken liver, cut into ½- to 1-inch-square pieces |
| 4 | tablespoons extra-virgin olive oil | | ¼ | cup pine nuts |
| 1 | medium onion, finely chopped | | ¼ | cup shelled pistachios, roughly chopped |
| ¼ | teaspoon ground allspice | | ¼ | cup currants (see page 31) |
| | Freshly ground pepper | | | |
| 2 ½ | cups water | | | |

Rinse the rice with a number of changes of cool water until the water runs clear. Place in a bowl, add 1 tablespoon of salt, and cover with warm water. Stir and allow to cool. Drain, rinse, and drain again.

In a large, heavy saucepan or pot over medium heat, heat the oil. Add the onion and cook until soft and translucent, about 10 minutes. Add the rice, season with the allspice, salt, and pepper, and stir to coat. Add the 2 ½ cups water and bring to a boil. Stir, cover with a tight-fitting lid, and cook over low heat without stirring or lifting the lid for 7 minutes. With a wide, round spatula, turn the rice over to ensure even cooking. Immediately replace the lid, and cook until the rice absorbs the liquid and is done but still firm, another 5 to 7 minutes depending on the rice. Check after 5 minutes.

If the rice is too moist, remove the lid; if it's too dry, sprinkle in some warm water. Remove from the heat.

Meanwhile, in a small saucepan over medium heat, melt the butter. Add the liver and pine nuts and cook until the liver is cooked through and the pine nuts are golden. Stir in the pistachios and currants. Remove from the heat.

Remove the lid from the rice and gently fold in the liver, pine nuts, pistachios, and currants with any remaining melted butter. Place a clean kitchen towel over the pot and replace the lid snuggly. Let sit in a warm corner of the kitchen for 40 minutes to 1 hour before serving.

With a large serving spoon, gently transfer the rice to a serving dish, taking care not to mash or break the rice.

# Spinach with Rice / Spanakorizo (Greece)

This unpretentious, filling dish is perfect during the numerous meatless days on the Greek Orthodox calendar. In winter, serve it warm as comfort food; in summer, serve it at room temperature with a bit more lemon.

| | | | | |
|---|---|---|---|---|
| 1 ¼ | pounds fresh spinach leaves | | ½ | teaspoon ground cumin |
| 4 | tablespoons extra-virgin olive oil | | | Salt and freshly ground pepper |
| 2 | medium onions, finely chopped | | 3 | sprigs fresh dill, 1 of them finely chopped |
| 1 | stalk celery, finely chopped | | 1 ½ | cups Vegetable Stock (page 35) or water |
| ¾ | cup long-grain rice | | | Juice of ½ small lemon |

Wash the spinach thoroughly in at least three changes of cold water. Shake off the excess water and tear into long shreds.

In a deep, heavy saucepan over medium heat, heat the oil. Add the onions and celery and cook until soft and translucent, about 10 minutes. Add the rice, cumin, and generous amounts of salt and pepper. Cook the rice for 2 minutes and then add the spinach and chopped dill. Stir well.

When the spinach begins to wilt, add the stock and lemon juice. Bring to a simmer, reduce the heat to low, cover, and cook without stirring until the rice is done but still firm and most of the water has been absorbed, about 15 minutes.

Remove the lid from the rice, place a clean kitchen towel over the pot, and replace the lid snugly. Let sit in a warm corner of the kitchen for 20 minutes before serving.

Before serving, garnish with the remaining 2 whole sprigs of dill.

# Leeks with Rice / Zeytinyağlı pırasa (Turkish Aegean)

This superb dish comes from a good friend and one-time next-door neighbor, Mustafa Varoglu. His family is Turkish with their (and this recipe's) roots in Ottoman-era Macedonia and Crete. Like many Turks, Mustafa (and his parents, Gonul and Erol) prepares several different olive oil–based vegetable dishes at once and then eats a little of each one over several days at the end of a meal, almost as a palate cleanser. This isn't a pilaf but a vegetable dish with, as Mustafa explains, "a handful of short-grain rice to absorb and concentrate the intense flavors, and give the textures a boost." It's served cool or at room temperature with plenty of bread and extra lemons to squeeze over the top. A dazzling end to any meal.

| | |
|---|---|
| 4 | tablespoons extra-virgin olive oil |
| 2 | pounds trimmed leeks (white and tender green parts only), cut into ½-inch-thick discs (7 to 8 cups) |
| 1 | carrot, cut into ¼-inch-thick discs (about 1 cup) |
| ¼ | teaspoon sugar |
| ¼ | cup short-grain rice |
| 2 | cups water |

| | |
|---|---|
| | Juice of 1 small lemon |
| 1 | teaspoon salt |
| | Freshly ground pepper |
| 2 | tablespoons finely chopped fresh flat-leaf parsley |
| 1 | lemon, cut into wedges |

In a large sauté pan or skillet over medium-low heat, heat the oil. Add the leeks, carrot, and sugar and cook until the leeks begin to sweat, 10 to 15 minutes.

Add the rice and cook, stirring frequently, for 1 minute.

Add the water, one-half of the lemon juice, and the salt. Bring to a boil, lower the heat, cover, and simmer until the rice is tender, stirring occasionally to make sure the rice cooks evenly, 15 to 18 minutes. There should be a little liquid left in the bottom of the pan to act as a sauce; sprinkle in some water if necessary.

Mix in the remaining lemon juice and then transfer to a serving dish to cool.

Grind some pepper over the top, garnish with parsley, and serve with the lemon wedges.

# White Rice with Vermicelli / Roz bil chariya (Lebanon-Syria-Egypt-Turkey)

In Lebanon, Syria, Egypt, and Turkey, white rice is cooked with short, thin strands of toasted pasta. It changes the texture and gives the rice an even nuttier flavor. It makes a wonderful accompaniment to meat, fish, and poultry dishes.

| | |
|---|---|
| 1 | cup long-grain rice |
| 2 | teaspoons butter |
| 1 | ounce vermicelli or angel-hair pasta, broken into ½- to 1-inch-long pieces (about ⅓ cup) |

| | |
|---|---|
| 2 ¼ | cups water |
| | Salt |

Rinse the rice with a number of changes of cool water until the water runs clear. Drain well.

In a heavy saucepan over medium heat, melt the butter. Add the vermicelli and cook, stirring frequently, until browned, about 3 minutes.

Stir in the rice, cover with the water, and season with salt. Bring to a boil, cover, reduce the heat to low, and cook until the liquid has been absorbed and the rice is tender, 12 to 15 minutes.

Fluff with a fork before serving.

# Upside-Down Rice and Eggplant Casserole / Ma'aloubet el batinjan (Syria)

This great Syrian recipe—layers of eggplant, spicy stewed meat, and rice inverted from the pan onto a plate before serving sprinkled with nuts and dolloped with yogurt—is adapted from one given to me by Georges Husni, the founding president of the Académie Syrienne de la Gastronomie in Aleppo. One of the world's oldest and greatest cities (and one of my very favorites), Aleppo is famous across the Arab world for its culinary traditions. It lies at the crossroads of several ancient trade routes, and goods passing from Antioch (modern-day Antakya) to Damascus, or Istanbul to Baghdad, or the Euphrates to the Mediterranean, have filled the splendid *souks* for thousands of years. But so have local goods from the fertile northern Syria landscape: I remember clearly one damp winter morning a decade ago traveling by bus from Antakya, on the southern Turkish Mediterranean coast to Aleppo, passing through groves of olives and nuts, orchards, rich red soil feathered with sharp greens, and flocks of grazing, fat-tailed Middle Eastern sheep.

| | | | | |
|---|---|---|---|---|
| 4 | tablespoons butter or ghee | | 3 ½ | cups water |
| 1 | pound stewing veal or lamb, cut into ½- to 1-inch cubes | | 3 | pounds eggplant |
| ½ | teaspoon sweet paprika | | | Olive oil for brushing |
| ½ | teaspoon ground cinnamon | | 1 ½ | cups long-grain rice |
| 2 | cardamom pods, crushed between the fingers | | ¼ | cup pine nuts |
| 2 | cloves | | ¼ | cup toasted almonds, skins slipped off |
| | Cayenne pepper | | 2 | cups thick natural yogurt |
| | Salt | | | |

In sauté pan or skillet over medium heat, melt the butter. Add the veal and cook until browned, 5 to 10 minutes. Add the paprika, cinnamon, cardamom, and cloves. Season with cayenne pepper and salt and cover with 1 cup of the water. Bring to a boil and cook over low heat for 45 minutes or until the meat is tender. Add more water if the mixture looks about to dry out as it cooks. Remove and discard the cloves and cardamom. Cover until ready to use.

Meanwhile, preheat the oven broiler.

Wash and stem the eggplant, and then peel lengthwise into ½- to ¾-inch-wide stripes, discarding the cut peels. Cut the eggplant crosswise into ½-inch-thick pieces. Lay on a baking sheet and brush with the olive oil. Place in the oven and broil until golden brown, 5 to 7 minutes. Turn over, brush with more oil, and broil until golden brown, 5 to 7 minutes.

Meanwhile, rinse the rice with a number of changes of cool water until the water runs clear. Place in a bowl, add 1 tablespoon of salt, and cover with warm water. Stir and allow to cool. Drain, rinse, drain again, and set aside.

In a 10-inch saucepan with sides at least 4 inches high, place a layer of half the eggplant at the bottom, followed by a layer of half the meat, and then a layer of half the rice. Gently press down. Repeat with the remaining eggplant, meat, and rice. Gently press down. Combine any leftover juice from the meat with water to make 3 cups; pour over the mixture. It should just cover the ingredients; add more if needed.

Bring to a boil, cover, reduce the heat to low, and simmer until the rice is tender, about 30 minutes. If all the liquid has evaporated and the rice is not done, sprinkle in additional water as needed.

Meanwhile, in a small sauté pan or skillet over low heat, dry roast the pine nuts and almonds until golden and fragrant, 6 to 8 minutes. Remove from the heat.

Remove the saucepan from the heat and let stand for 15 minutes. Cover the pan snugly with a plate and invert. Tap on the pan to release the casserole. Unmold carefully. Sprinkle the dry-roasted nuts over the casserole. Serve with the yogurt.

## **Pigeon Stuffed with Rice / Hamam mahshi** (Egypt)

Earthen, tapering pigeon *cotes*, or coops, with protruding stick perches sprout up in tight pairs across Egypt's Nile Delta, weighing down garages, shops, and simple brick homes. Nowhere have I eaten such tender, juicy pigeons—grilled as well as stuffed with either rice or *frik* (green wheat)—as in Egypt in springtime. Squab or poussins make perfect substitutions. Lovely served on a bed of greens (such as arugula, as at the incomparable Abou El Sid restaurant in Cairo), the stuffed birds are eaten with the fingers, so serve with finger bowls of water, a lemon wedge, and a few sprigs of mint.

| | |
|---|---|
| 4 | fledgling pigeons, squabs, or small poussins (about 1 pound each), cleaned, livers reserved |
| | Salt and freshly ground pepper |
| 3 | tablespoons butter |
| 1 | medium onion, finely chopped |
| 6 | cardamom seeds, slightly crushed |
| | Ground allspice |
| ¾ | cup short- or medium-grain rice, preferably Baldo |
| ⅓ | cup water |
| 1 | three-inch piece cinnamon stick |
| 1 | mastic tear, crushed with a pinch of sugar just before adding (see page 209) |
| 1 | bay leaf |

Wash the birds. Pat dry with paper towels. Generously season the outside as well as the cavities with salt and pepper.

In a sauté pan or skillet over medium heat, melt 2 tablespoons of the butter. Add the onion and cook until soft and translucent, about 10 minutes. Roughly chop the livers and add to the pan, along with 4 of the cardamom seeds, a generous pinch of allspice, and the rice. Cook, stirring continuously, for 2 minutes, until the liver is browned and the ingredients mixed. Add ⅓ cup water, cover, and cook, stirring frequently, until the water has been absorbed. Transfer the rice to a bowl until it is cool enough to be handled with your fingers.

Stuff the pigeons with the rice mixture. Loosely fill the breast cavity as well as the neck cavity to no more than three-fourths full. Without ripping the skin, gently lift the skin away from the breast and stuff some of the rice mixture in the breast and back areas. Pull the skin back over the cavities and secure closed with toothpicks. Truss the legs.

In a wide, heavy pot, Dutch oven, or sauté pan or skillet, lay the pigeons breast-side down; they should be close but not touching. Pour enough water around the birds to cover them at least halfway up. Add the remaining 1 tablespoon of butter and remaining 2 cardamom seeds, the cinnamon stick, mastic, and bay leaf. Bring to a gentle boil, reduce the heat to low, cover, and cook for 1 hour. Turn the birds breast-side up 30 minutes into the cooking time.

Meanwhile, preheat the oven to 350°F.

Carefully transfer the birds to a baking dish. Bake until golden, about 15 minutes. Serve breast-side up.

# Alexandria-Style Amber Rice with Fish / Sayadeya (Alexandria, Egypt)

On weekends, local families and day-tripping ones from Cairo crowd into seafood restaurants along Alexandria's long, arching waterfront Corniche and the fishermen's quarter of the Anfushi district. At Kadoura, a local favorite, diners choose from a selection of the day's catch—red mullet, crab, sea bass, bream, squid, bluefish, jumbo prawns—and then climb the stairs to find a table. A spread of "salads"—hummus, baba ghanoush, tahini, *bessara*—comes while the fish or seafood cooks to perfection. One night here last spring, the waiter brought my fish along with a classic local fisherman's rice, amber colored and cooked and served in a round terra-cotta dish called a *bram*. (The color comes from slowly darkened onions. The trick is to bring them to a dark hue without burning, which will make the rice bitter.) My version here has pieces of fish on top to make it more substantial, though that night at Kadoura I had it plain to accompany the platter of tin-red, cumin-rubbed grilled red mullet.

| | | | |
|---|---|---|---|
| 1 | pound firm white-fleshed fish fillets, such as sea bream, sea bass, or snapper, cut into 3- to 4-inch pieces | 5 | cups water |
| | Salt and freshly ground pepper | 2 | cups short- or medium-grain rice |
| 4 | tablespoons olive oil | ¾ | teaspoon ground cumin |
| 2 | medium onions, finely chopped | 1 | mastic tear, crushed with pinch of sugar just before adding (see page 209) |
| 2 | garlic cloves, minced | 2 | cardamom pods, lightly crushed |

Generously season the fish with salt and pepper.

In a terra-cotta bram, casserole, or heavy sauté pan or skillet over medium heat, heat the oil. Lay in the fish and fry, turning only once, until golden. Transfer to a paper towel–lined plate.

In the same oil, add the onions, reduce the heat to low, partly cover, and cook, stirring frequently, until rich brown but not burnt, about 30 minutes. Watch very carefully, especially at the end. Add the garlic and cook during the 2 final minutes.

Add the water and bring to a boil; the water should be the color of weak black tea. Add the rice, cumin, mastic, and cardamom; cook uncovered over medium heat for 10 minutes until the water is largely absorbed.

Break the fish into bite-sized pieces and lay on top of the rice. Taste the rice for seasoning and adjust as needed. Cover and cook over low heat for 8 to 10 minutes until the rice is done. The final texture of the rice should be firm, shiny, moist, and the color of amber.

Serve in a terra-cotta bram.

# Marinated Fish Stuffed with Rice and Black Olives / Poisson mariné farci au riz et aux olives noires (Morocco)

Wedged between ocean and sea, Morocco has the luxury of selling extremely fresh seafood from both the Atlantic Ocean and the Mediterranean Sea in its markets. The tangy flavors of this fish dish come from the *charmoula* marinade. There's plenty of chunky tomato, olive, and rice filling—it not only fills the fish but spills out around it.

| | |
|---|---|
| 2 or 3 whole sea bream, sea bass, or porgy (2½ to 3 pounds total) | 1 pound tomatoes, seeded and finely chopped, juices reserved |
| ½ cup Moroccan Fish Marinade (page 86) | 4 ounces pitted black olives, roughly chopped |
| Salt | ½ cup warm water |
| ½ cup long-grain rice | |

Clean the fish, completely emptying out the cavity. Rinse well and pat dry with paper towels. Make a parallel set of hash marks—cutting to the bone — in both sides of the fish.

Place the fish in a large baking dish and coat with ¼ cup of the marinade, rubbing it into the cuts and the cavity. Cover, refrigerate, and marinate for at least 1 hour.

In a medium pot, bring an abundant amount of water to a boil. Add 2 pinches of salt and the rice and boil for 10 minutes. Drain the rice but do not rinse.

Preheat the oven to 350°F.

Transfer the rice to a large bowl. Add the remaining ¼ cup of marinade along with the tomatoes and olives and mix thoroughly.

Place the fish in a roasting pan. Stuff with as much of the mixture as possible; spread the remaining mixture around the fish. Drizzle the ½ cup of warm water over the fish and stuffing.

Bake in the oven until the fish are just done, 20 to 50 minutes depending on the size of fish, basting from time to time.

Peel away the skin and gently lift off the fillets from the fish; serve with the stuffing alongside. Spoon over top any juice from the pan.

## Moroccan Fish Marinade / Charmoula

Charmoula can include different spices, but I have learned not to experiment too much with it, or at least not to say anything if I do. After I casually mentioned adding onions and saffron to a recent version, one Moroccan cook emphatically told me: "Charmoula for fish has no onions nor saffron. For chicken, yes, but fish, never!"

| | |
|---|---|
| ¼ | cup finely chopped fresh flat-leaf parsley |
| ¼ | cup finely chopped fresh cilantro |
| 2 | garlic cloves, minced |
| 1 | teaspoon sweet paprika (piment doux) |
| 1 | teaspoon ground cumin |
| ½ | teaspoon salt |
| ¼ | teaspoon cayenne pepper (piment fort) |
| ¼ | cup extra-virgin olive oil |
| | Juice of ½ lemon |

Add all of the ingredients in a large bowl. Mix until thoroughly blended.

Use within 2 days while the colors remain bright.

To store, lay plastic wrap across the surface of the bowl and keep in the refrigerator.

# Creamy Vanilla-Scented Rice Pudding / Rizogalo (Greece)

Rice pudding is one of the few universal rice dishes around the entire Mediterranean. But that doesn't mean these sweet, milky desserts are similar. Each regional version has its distinctive flavors.

I've adapted this creamy Greek recipe, passed from mother to daughter for generations, from Dora Zerwoodis, whose family comes from the island of Andros and some of the other northern Cyclades. Each year she gathers with a group of her sisters, cousins, and nieces at the family beach house in Rafina, outside Athens, to talk and cook. There is always rice pudding in the refrigerator. Dora doesn't add raisins to her version, although some of her cousins in Athens do. Here they're optional.

| | | | | |
|---|---|---|---|---|
| ½ | cup water | | ½ | cup sugar |
| ½ | cup short-grain rice | | 1 | teaspoon pure vanilla extract |
| 4 | cups whole milk | | 1 | large egg, at room temperature |
| ½ | cup seedless raisins, rinsed (optional) | | | Cinnamon for dusting |

In a saucepan over high heat, add the water and rice, stir, and bring to a boil. Boil uncovered until the water is mostly absorbed, about 2 minutes. Add the milk and the raisins (if using). Bring to a boil, reduce the heat to low, and simmer uncovered for 30 minutes, stirring periodically to break any skin that forms and to prevent sticking.

Increase the heat to medium, stir in the sugar and vanilla, return the mixture to a boil, and boil for 3 minutes, stirring frequently. Remove from the heat.

In a medium bowl, whisk the egg. Very slowly mix in 1 cup of the rice mixture, stirring constantly. Pour the rice-egg mixture into the pot and stir until thoroughly blended.

Divide the rice among 6 parfait or dessert glasses.

Let cool to room temperature. Cover with plastic wrap and refrigerate until chilled. Just before serving, liberally dust with cinnamon.

## Oven-Baked Rice Pudding with Mastic / Sakızlı fırın sütlaç (Turkey)

The first time I went to Istanbul, I planned to stay all winter. It was 1994, and I had been traveling almost nonstop for three years. It was a step toward settling down; I had just applied to graduate school in England and would begin the following autumn.

The weather was cold and wet, and low, charcoal clouds hovered over the city. Much of my time was spent in cafes and *muhallebici*, "dairy bars" specializing in milky puddings. Creamy, baked rice pudding was a discovery for me, especially when flavored with mastic. Crushed tears of mastic give a piney flavor to the pudding and a chewier consistency. But two weeks of steady rain and gray skies pummeled my mood and even such luxurious and delicious rice puddings couldn't hold me any longer. I headed south looking for sun, drifting through Turkey and Syria and Jordan, finding it, at last, months later, in the Sinai Penninsula. But by then, I was missing Istanbul (and rice puddings), and though the sun was shining, I began heading back north.

| | | | | |
|---|---|---|---|---|
| 1 | cup water | | ½ | cup sugar |
| ⅓ | cup short-grain rice | | 1 | small mastic tear, crushed with pinch of sugar just before adding (see page 209) |
| | Salt | | 2 | egg yolks |
| 4 | cups whole milk, plus more as needed | | 1 | tablespoon butter, cut into small pieces |
| 2 | tablespoons rice flour | | | |

In a large, heavy saucepan over high heat, bring the water to a boil. Add the rice and a pinch of salt and boil until the water is just absorbed.

Meanwhile, in another saucepan over medium heat, warm 1 cup of the milk. Add the rice flour and whisk until the flour is dissolved and there are no lumps.

Add the rice-flour mixture to the rice pan along with the remaining 3 cups of milk and the sugar. Bring to a simmer, lower the heat, and cook, stirring frequently, until the rice is chewy and tender and the mixture is creamy and thickened, 35 to 40 minutes. The consistency should be soupy; add more milk if needed.

Add the mastic and cook, stirring constantly, over the lowest heat, for a final 2 to 3 minutes. Taste for sweetness and stir in more sugar if desired.

Preheat the broiler and set the oven rack 5 to 6 inches from the element.

Place the egg yolks and butter in a medium bowl. Skim off a scant ¼ cup of milky liquid from the pudding, add to the yolks and butter and whisk together.

Divide the pudding among 4 to 6 ovenproof ramekins or deep dessert bowls. Spoon the egg mixture over the tops, place the ramekins on a baking sheet, and place into the oven. Broil until the top is motley brown, 3 to 5 minutes.

Let cool to room temperature. Cover with plastic wrap and refrigerate until chilled. Remove just before serving.

# Spiced Rice-Flour Pudding / Moghli (Lebanon)

In Lebanon, families prepare this caraway-and-anise-laden rice-flour pudding for guests after the birth of a baby. It's a laborious dish that needs to be stirred constantly. Tiring work when it is prepared for the full requisite forty days. . . .

| | | | | |
|---|---|---|---|---|
| 1 | cup rice flour | | 1 | teaspoon anise seeds, ground |
| 6 | cups cold water | | ½ | teaspoon ground cinnamon |
| 1 ¼ | cups sugar | | ½ | cup shelled pistachios, coarsely chopped |
| 1 | teaspoon caraway seeds, ground | | | |

In a heavy saucepan over low heat, gently heat the rice flour and water, stirring vigorously until the flour is dissolved and there are no lumps. Add the sugar, caraway, anise, and cinnamon. Cook, stirring frequently and not allowing anything to stick to the pan, until the mixture thickens to the consistency of pudding, about 30 minutes.

Divide the pudding among 6 to 8 parfait glasses.

Let cool to room temperature. Cover with plastic wrap and refrigerate until chilled. Garnish with the pistachios before serving.

# Baked Apples with Rice Meringue /
# Pommes au riz meringuées (Provence, France)

A couple of times a year, Eva, the girls, and I go to Marseille to stay with close friends. Pascal is French, Valeria is Argentinean, and they have two young daughters whose ages mirror, within weeks, our two. They live in a converted farmhouse and stable outside the city on the road to Cassis. In the summer we eat on the terrace that faces an immense field of wild grasses and herbs—rosemary, thyme, asparagus, fennel—backed by a massive bowl of white stone mountains; in the winter we eat inside around a low table beside the fireplace. The inspiration, and initial clues, for this sweet dessert—essentially *pommes meringuées* set on a layer of rice pudding—comes from one of the two well-thumbed cookbooks that Pascal routinely consults, J.B. Reboul's 19th-century *La cuisinière provençale*. This is a treat eaten next to a simmering fire.

| | |
|---|---|
| 2 ½ | cups whole milk |
| ⅔ | cup short- or medium-grain rice |
| 3 | tablespoons butter |
| ½ | cup plus 2 tablespoons sugar |
| ¼ | teaspoon vanilla extract |

| | |
|---|---|
| 3 | Granny Smith, Fuji, or Golden Delicious apples, peeled, quartered, seeded, and cut into ½-inch-thick slices |
| 2 | tablespoons white wine |
| 2 | egg whites |
| ½ | cup superfine (castor) sugar |

In a saucepan over medium-high heat, bring the milk to a gentle boil. Add the rice and cook, stirring occasionally, for 10 minutes. Stir in 1 tablespoon of the butter, the ½ cup sugar, and the vanilla, and cook for another 15 minutes or until the rice is chewy and creamy. Spread the rice out on a 9-inch-round ovenproof pie pan.

In a large sauté pan or skillet over medium heat, melt the remaining 2 tablespoons of butter. Add the apples, cover with the remaining 2 tablespoons of sugar, and cook, stirring gently from time to time, until the apples begin to soften, about 5 minutes. Splash in the wine and continue to cook until the apples are golden and soft but not mushy.

Preheat the oven to 350°F.

In a clean copper, stainless-steel, or glass mixing bowl, use a hand mixer to whisk the egg whites on low to medium speed until frothy and foamy. Gradually add the sugar, increase the speed, and beat to shiny, medium peaks.

Arrange the apples over the rice and cover completely with a thick layer of the meringue. Bake in the oven for about 15 minutes or until the meringue is golden.

Cut into pielike wedges and serve.

# pasta

# Mediterranean Pasta Primer

## Brief History and Overview

Pasta's Mediterranean origins are widely debated. The Romans grew soft wheat, which is more suitable for fresh pasta and bread. But dried pasta? Dried pasta's genesis is in the advent of hard durum wheat. With high gluten and low moisture content, durum wheat semolina makes perfect pasta: it can be stored for long periods of time, and it holds its shape and texture when boiled. Food historian Clifford Wright makes a comprehensive case in *The Mediterranean Feast* that it wasn't the Etruscans, Chinese, Greeks, or Romans, but the Arabs who introduced pasta after conquering Spain in the 8th century and Sicily in the 9th century.

What is clear, though, is that it was the Italians who created an entire culture around pasta; it stands as one of their greatest culinary achievements.

Dried pasta (*pasta secca*) was eaten only by the elite as a handmade specialty until around the 15th century, when commercial production began. This centered in Sicily and around Naples in the Campania region, which have the long, hot, dry summers and mild winters necessary for growing durum wheat, as well as the ideal mix of inland winds and warm sea breezes for drying pasta. By the early 17th century, industrialized techniques made pasta available to all classes, pasta shops flourished, and it was embraced as part of daily life in southern Italy.

Dried pasta, though, wasn't a widespread staple in the north of the country until World War II, nor did northern farmers even grow durum wheat. This part of Italy, above all in the Emilia-Romagna region, is the heartland of fresh egg pasta (*pasta fresca* or *pasta all'uovo*), made with softer flour wheat.

Pasta is eaten everywhere in the Mediterranean. The pasta itself is often imported from Italy, the Italian names for shapes are used, and some of the accompanying sauces are similar. But this is not always the case. There's a wide range of what I call "indigenous pastas"— pastas that retain a distinctive local form, preparation technique, or cooking tradition.

In coastal Croatia, for instance, just across the Adriatic Sea from Italy and for centuries largely under Venetian rule, Croatians eat plenty of spaghetti (with tomato sauce, with seafood, with squid ink), but also *mlinci*, fresh pasta rolled into sheets and baked until crispy. It's broken into pieces, rehydrated, and stirred into the drippings of, most famously, roast turkey.

While pasta is found across Spain, only Catalonia, Valencia, and Alicante created their own culinary traditions with it. One of the most delectable is short, thin *fideo* noodles treated like rice, absorbing and swelling with the flavors of the pan. Introduced by Arabs a millenium ago and found in medieval recipe books, fideos have long been an important part of the cuisine here. Cooked in a *cazuela* (terra-cotta casserole), the inland version includes a tomato sauce chunky with pork ribs and nuggets of fresh pork sausage, while the coastal version cooks in a wide paella pan with the flavors of the sea.

Greece is one of the world's top pasta consumers, though Greeks tend to eat little variety in shapes. One favorite shape is *kritharaki* (orzo), tossed simply with brown butter and hard goat's cheese or sprinkled into casseroles to suck up the flavors. Cooking the pasta right in the sauce is not at all uncommon. Greece also boasts some unique pastas, including sweet-and-sour versions of *trahana*, a hard, pebblelike pasta made with milk or yogurt.

In Egypt, Lebanon, Syria, and Turkey, short, thin pasta noodles are frequently cooked with white rice. In Turkey the most famous pasta is *mantı*, tiny stuffed "packets" made with soft flour. This ancient dish most likely originated in Central Asia but was found in the royal kitchens of Ottoman Turkey by the 15th century. Commonly stuffed with a pinch of spiced meat, they're served topped with garlicky yogurt, a dribble of melted butter, and dusted in sumac and dried mint.

Both Tunisia—a mere eighty-seven miles from Italy—and Libya—which was an Italian colony from 1911 to 1943—consume vast amounts of macaroni and spaghetti dishes, while small noodles are found in potages and soups across North Africa. Flat, orzolike *tlitli* in Algeria and short, vermicelli-thin *chariya* in Morocco are treated like couscous and steamed in a couscoussier. *Chariya* is also sweetened and eaten not as a dessert but as a dinner dish either on its own or, more elaborately, burying a whole braised chicken (similar to Braised Chicken Buried in Sweet Couscous on page 192). Sumptuous. And for fresh pasta, two regional favorites include a ginger-and-cinnamon chicken *tajine* topped with a bird's nest of egg noodles (memorably eaten one winter evening in an old northern Moroccan farmhouse), and thin, short Algerian *rechta* (made with durum wheat and water) that is first steamed in a couscoussier before being doused with earthy chicken-and-turnip-laden broth.

## Matching Pastas with Sauces

Certain shapes pair best with certain sauces. As a general rule, thinner strands and smaller shapes go best with light, delicate, and thinner sauces; broader strands, tubes, and sturdy shapes with hearty or meaty sauces; twisty shapes with creamy sauces; wide ribbons and square sheets (flat or rolled into tubes for stuffing) for baking; and small shapes for broths, stews, and soups.

Dried and fresh pasta also differ in their optimal pairings. Dried pasta combines well with robust tomato- or oil-based sauces, while fresh egg pasta with more delicate sauces, often based on butter, cream, cheese, or broth.

## Key Regional Pastas and Shapes

There are hundreds of pasta shapes around the Mediterranean. Even outside Italy, many retain their Italian name. Suffixes and adjectives denote different sizes: *-ine*, *-ini*, *-ette*, and *-etti* means "small" or "thin"; *-one* and *-oni* mean "large." For different surfaces: *lisce* and *lisci* mean "smooth" while *rigate* and *rigati* mean "ridged." I have left out many of the better-known, universal shapes, such as spaghetti, tagliatelle, penne, fettuccine, fusilli, etc. Unless otherwise stated, the most common form of the pastas listed below is dried.

**AGNOLOTTI:** Ravioli-like filled fresh pasta from Piedmont. Fillings blend boiled and cured meats with Swiss chard, escarole, or another vegetable. Usually served in broth or tossed with melted butter.

**BUCATINI:** Long hollow strands slightly chunkier than spaghetti. In Greece they are cooked in casseroles. Also called *perciatelli*.

**BUSIATE:** Long, hollow strands from Sicily slightly thicker than bucatini.

**CANNELLONI:** Flat, 2 1/2- to 3-inch-square sheets boiled and then rolled into stuffed tubes. Substitute lasagna sheets broken to size.

**CAPPELLETTI:** Filled pasta folded into the shape of a little hat; from Modena in the Emilia-Romagna region of Italy. Similar to tortellini.

**CHARIYA:** *see Fideos*

**CONCHIGLIE:** The concave shape of these small conch shells traps sauces.

**ELICHE:** Short, screw-shaped pasta similar to fusilli, but with tighter spirals.

**FIDEOS** (*fideus* in Catalan): Short, thin noodles from Spain used in soups but also stewed in casseroles. They come in five sizes: Number 0 is as fine as angel-hair pasta and takes just 2 minutes to cook (best for soups), while Number 4 is as thick as spaghetti and cooks in 11 minutes (best for casseroles). Turkish *şehriye* are similar to very fine, 1-inch-long fideos and are used in certain pilaf dishes as well as in soups. Moroccan chariya noodles are also about 1 inch in length, though they're often treated like couscous and steamed in a couscoussier. To substitute any of these variations, break or cut long, thin pasta such as angel hair, vermicelli, or tagliarini (tagliolini) into 1/2- to 1-inch lengths.

**FREGOLA:** *see* Mediterranean Couscous Primer, page 159

**FUŽI:** From the Istrian Peninsula in northern Croatia, this fresh pasta is 1- to 1 1/2- inch square or diamond-shaped pieces of pasta, folded in half from opposite corners and pinched to form simple tubes or loose bows.

**GALETS DE NADAL:** Large, snail-shaped ridged shells made of durum wheat and egg from Catalonia. Standard ones measure about 1 1/4 inches square, though there are smaller-sized ones as well. Similar to Italian *lumache rigate*.

**HILOPITES:** Fresh flat Greek egg noodles that are sometimes long but are most often cut into diamond shapes.

**KRITHARAKI:** *see Orzo*

**LANGUES D'OISEAUX:** *see Orzo*

**MALLOREDDUS:** Sardinian ridged and oblong pasta with curled-in bottom edges. Sometimes the pasta is made with saffron, though this yellowish tint can be duplicated by dropping threads of saffron into the water when boiling. Also called *gnocchetti sardi*, "little Sardinian gnocchi."

**MANESTRA:** *see Orzo*

**MANTI:** Tiny stuffed Turkish pasta shaped like little bags. About as big around as a penny, a dozen or so fit onto a large soup spoon. Occasionally triangular shaped.

**MLINCI:** Fresh Croatian pasta rolled out into sheets and baked in the oven until crispy. To serve, break into pieces, rehydrate with hot water, and then cook in the drippings of roasted poultry.

**NWASSER:** Fresh Tunisian pasta cut into small squares.

**ORECCHIETTE:** "Little ears." Wonderful, chewy dime-sized discs from Puglia.

**ORZO:** Tiny, barely shaped pasta with a lovely buttery texture. One of the most common pastas in Greece, where it's also known as *kritharaki* and *manestra*. In

North Africa, short, flattish, orzo-shaped pasta are called *langues d'oiseaux* ("birds' tongues"); in Algeria they are also called *tlitli*.

**PAPPARDELLE:** These wide, flat egg noodles originally from Tuscany are 3/4 to 1 inch wide and can be bought both fresh and dried, and either straight edged or fluted.

**RECHTA:** Fresh Algerian noodles made from hard durum semolina and water, cut into skinny ribbons, and steamed in the top of a couscoussier. Substitute broken vermicelli.

**ŞEHRIYE:** *see Fideos*

**ŠTRUKLI:** Fresh Croatian filled pasta that originated from around Zagreb but is now found around the country. There are two main forms: similar to ravioli; and layered, stuffed sheets rolled into a long, fat coil, boiled, and then baked.

**TLITLI:** *see Orzo*

**TORTELLINI:** Although the most popular dried stuffed pasta, these plump, round rings from Bologna are also prepared fresh, especially at Christmas, when they are filled with ground prosciutto, mortadella, and either capon or pork, and eaten in capon broth. Supposedly inspired by Venus' navel.

**TRAHANA:** A hard, pebble-sized Greek pasta made in a sweet form with fresh milk and in a sour form with yogurt. Often crumbled into soups or stews.

**VERMICELLI:** Long, very fine noodles sometimes sold coiled in delicate nests. They can be crumbled as a substitute for fideos, chariya, or şehriye.

**ZITI:** Long, thick, hollow tubes are broken into desired lengths.

## Mediterranean Pasta Cheeses

**EMMENTAL:** A buttery cow's milk cheese sprinkled over Spanish pastas and grated on top of stuffed cannelloni for a gratin. Similar to "Swiss cheese."

**ĠBEJNA:** This small, round goat's or sheep's milk cheese from Malta comes in various forms. The hard, salted variety is excellent grated over pasta.

**GRANA PADANO:** A rich, grainy, hard Italian cheese produced mainly in Italy's Lombardy region from cow's milk. It's aged up to eighteen months and is milder and less salty than Parmigiano-Reggiano.

**KASSERI:** A pale yellow Greek cheese that ranges from mild- to sharp-tasting. Good for sprinkling over pasta.

**KEFALOTIRI:** This aged, hard yellow Greek cheese made with sheep's or goat's milk is excellent grated over pasta. Rich, tangy, and very salty, it's similar to Pecorino Romano.

**MIZITHRA:** This Greek cheese made from the leftover whey in making feta comes both fresh and unsalted—similar to ricotta and sometimes used in baking—and dried. The dried variation is egg-shaped and nutty, and excellent over pasta.

**PARMIGIANO-REGGIANO:** Considered the king of the Italian cheeses for its lush, nutty flavor and fine texture. Produced in the Emilia-Romagna region, it's aged for eighteen months up to more than thirty. The cheese of choice for grating over pasta dishes as well as stirring into risottos.

**PECORINO:** There are two main types of this hard, salty sheep's milk cheese: Pecorino Romano (from the Lazio region, near Rome) and the sharper Pecorino Sardo (from the Sardinia area).

**RICOTTA:** A fresh, very soft white cheese made from the leftover whey of sheep's milk cheese.

**RICOTTA SALATA:** A firm, aged ricotta from southern Italy that's saltier than Parmigiano-Reggiano, Grana Padano, and pecorino.

## Making Fresh Pasta

Fresh pasta dough needs to be stretched, not compressed, to its desired thinness. Although generally made using soft flour—the best is Italian *farina tipo* "00" (*doppio zero*)—and eggs, certain North African fresh pastas use hard durum semolina flour and just a touch of water. Pasta is best rolled in a humid kitchen; put a tea kettle or pot of water on to boil while working. In Tuscany, many chefs add olive oil to the dough to make it even more supple.

### Techniques and Secrets

#### PANS AND UTENSILS
The pasta pot should be made of lightweight metal (to allow the water to come to a fast boil) and large; pasta for 4 people needs 4 quarts of water. Giving the pasta plenty of room keeps it from sticking together as well as space to grow. Moreover, the water will return to a boil faster once the pasta has been added. The pot should have two handles to hold while draining the boiled pasta into a large colander.

#### AMOUNTS
The standard amount of pasta for 4 people as a main course (or 6 as a first course) is 14 ounces, or 3 1/2 ounces (100 grams) per person.

#### BOILING PASTA
Bring the water to a boil and add salt. When the water returns to a rolling boil, add the pasta all at once. Return the water quickly to a boil. Stir frequently to keep the pasta from sticking together, especially at the beginning when starch thickly coats the surface. Cook delicate stuffed pastas at a simmer, not a boil.

#### SALTING THE WATER
Salting the boiling water seasons the pasta as it cooks. If seasoned correctly, the sauce will require less salt. Use 1 teaspoon of salt per 1 quart of water.

#### FINDING AL DENTE
Literally meaning "to the tooth," *al dente* is the ideal state of doneness when pasta is firm but not brittle, tender and slightly springy, not mushy. Test frequently, beginning about 2 or 3 minutes before the suggested cooking time on the package.

#### DRAINING
Drain the pasta into a large colander. Shake and swirl the colander to drain any remaining pasta water. Do not rinse! The surface starch helps the sauce cling to the pasta.

#### BLENDING WITH SAUCE
Blend the sauce with the pasta immediately to prevent the pasta from sticking together. Hot pasta also better absorbs sauce. Return the drained pasta to the still-warm pot where it boiled, add the sauce, and mix well before turning it out into a large serving bowl.

# Fresh Egg Pasta

For 5 to 6 servings, use 3 cups of flour, 4 eggs, and 2 tablespoons of oil.

| | |
|---|---|
| 2 ¼ cups tipo "oo" flour or American unbleached all-purpose flour (about 10 ½ ounces), plus more for dusting | 3 large eggs, at room temperature<br>1 ½ tablespoons extra-virgin olive oil (optional) |

On a large, clean working surface, mound the flour and make a well. Crack the eggs into the center and pour over the oil (if using). Beat the eggs with a fork and then begin mixing in flour from the sides, gradually incorporating it all into a single ball.

Scrape the surface clean and lightly flour. Patiently knead the dough for 10 minutes until supple and silky. Work in a bit of flour or some drops of cold water if necessary.

Wrap the dough in plastic wrap and let rest for 30 minutes to 1 hour.

Break off one-third or one-fourth of the dough; rewrap the rest in plastic until ready to use.

To roll using a pasta machine: Securely fasten the machine to the edge of a table and open the rollers to their widest setting. Press the ball into a flat disc and then run it through the rollers. Fold the dough in half and run it through the rollers again. Tighten the rollers a notch and run it through them. Continue stepping down notches until reaching the desired thickness. Cut the pasta in half if it becomes unwieldy long.

To hand-roll: Press the ball into a flat disc and begin rolling it with a long wooden dowel. Roll away from the center, stretching the dough outward, and working until reaching the desired thickness.

Cut the stretched sheet into the desired shape or width, 5-by-6-inch rectangles for lasagna, $1^{1}/_{4}$- to $1^{1}/_{2}$-inch squares for tortellini or cappelletti, and so on. For pappardelle, cut the sheet with a pasta wheel, pizza cutter, or sharp knife into $^{3}/_{4}$- to 1-inch-wide strips.

For long ribbons of pasta, run the sheet back through the machine to be cut into tagliatelle (or fettuccine) or thinner tagliarini. To cut by hand, flour both sides of the stretched sheet and loosely roll up into a cylinder. Using a sharp knife, cut $^{1}/_{4}$-inch-wide strips for tagliatelle, $^{1}/_{16}$-inch-wide or so for spaghetti, and so on. Gently open the rolls.

Douse the cut strands with flour to keep them from sticking together and gently lay on a floured dish towel or in a large, floured baking pan.

Repeat the process with the remaining dough, keeping the unused portion wrapped and the cut pieces floured.

Let dry for 30 minutes before using.

# PASTA RECIPES

# Lentil Chorba / Chorba aux lentilles (Algiers, Algeria)

It's dark in Algiers by 6 PM in December, and even though the days are often dazzlingly sunny, the evenings chill quickly in the Mediterranean dampness. A previous winter, with unbroken repetition, my dinners there began with *chorba* or *hrira*, two types of thick, nourishing vegetable- and legume-filled soup. The best were at Restaurant El Djenina, a forty-year-old bastion of traditional Algerian cooking. Though the ceilings of the hundred-year-old palace that houses El Djenina are high and ornate, the walls covered with decorative antique tiles, and many of the dishes elaborate, their lentil soup is downright homey. Flavored with lamb and laced with plenty of fresh herbs and sharp spices, I couldn't resist refilling my large bowl three times from the tureen on the table. Warmed and revived, I was ready for the main course: a sweet tajine of lamb and prunes; or a large whole fish, chosen earlier from a tray of the day's catch, prepared in the oven; or the house specialty couscous with lamb, meatballs, and caramelized onions. . . . But first—always first—was soup. And after a week of winter Algiers nights, I understood why.

| | |
|---|---|
| 2 | tablespoons extra-virgin olive oil |
| 8 | ounces veal stewing meat, cut into ½-inch cubes |
| 1 | medium onion, finely chopped |
| 2 | tomatoes, peeled, seeded, and finely chopped |
| 2 | tablespoons tomato concentrate |
| 8 | ounces dried brown lentils (scant 1 ½ cups), rinsed |
| 1 | teaspoon sweet paprika (piment doux) |
| 2 | pinches cayenne pepper (piment fort) |

| | |
|---|---|
| | Salt and freshly ground pepper |
| 7 | cups water |
| ¼ | cup chariya, fideos, or crumbled vermicelli or angel-hair pasta |
| 2 | tablespoons finely chopped fresh flat-leaf parsley |
| 1 | lemon, cut into wedges |
| | Harissa (optional; see page 165) |

In a large, heavy saucepan or pot over medium heat, heat the oil. Add the veal and onion and cook, stirring frequently, until the meat is browned and the onion begins to soften, about 5 minutes.

Add the tomatoes, tomato concentrate, and lentils; sprinkle in the paprika and cayenne pepper; and season with salt and a generous amount of pepper. Cover with the water, bring to a boil, reduce the heat, cover, and simmer until the lentils are tender, 30 to 40 minutes.

Scoop out 1 cup of the lentils (without pieces of meat), purée it or pass it through a food mill, and then return it to the soup. Add the pasta and cook until tender. Add more liquid if needed to keep the soup runny. Taste for seasoning and adjust as needed.

Stir in the parsley and serve the soup in wide bowls with lemon wedges to squeeze over the top and harissa (if using) to stir in as desired.

# Pasta and White Bean Soup / Pasta e fagioli (Italy)

Tuscan cooks often prefer this classic bean-and-pasta soup with cannellini beans, the small white kidney beans with a smooth texture and nutty flavor, while their counterparts elsewhere in northern Italy may use slightly sweet, splotchy pinkish-brown *borlotti* (cranberry beans). Stirring in butter and cheese at the end adds a soothing lushness.

The dish is sometimes referred to as "pasta fazool," as Dean Martin so fittingly sang:

> *When the stars make you drool*
> *Just like pasta fazool*
> *That's amore.*

| | |
|---|---|
| 1 ½ | cup dried cannellini or borlotti beans (about 10 ounces) |
| ¼ | cup extra-virgin olive oil |
| 1 | medium onion, finely chopped |
| ½ | carrot, finely chopped |
| ½ | stalk celery with leaves, finely chopped |
| 1 | garlic clove, minced |
| 1 | tablespoon finely chopped fresh flat-leaf parsley |

| | |
|---|---|
| 3 | ounces lean cured pancetta, cut into ¼-inch cubes |
| 1 | cup canned Italian plum tomatoes, finely chopped, all juices reserved |
| | Salt and freshly ground pepper |
| 8 | cups low-sodium beef stock |
| 1 ½ | cup ditali or other small, hollow soup pasta (about 4 ounces) |
| 2 | tablespoons butter |
| 1 ½ | ounces freshly grated Parmigiano-Reggiano |

Soak the beans overnight in abundant water. Drain and rinse.

Put the beans in a large pot. Cover with plenty of fresh cool water, bring to a boil, and cook at a gentle boil until the beans are tender but not mushy, about 45 minutes, depending on size and age of the beans. Remove from the heat. Drain only when ready to add to the soup.

Meanwhile, prepare a soffritto. In a large, heavy saucepan or pot over medium-low heat, heat the oil, add the onion, and cook until it begins to soften, about 5 minutes. Add the carrot, celery, garlic, parsley, and pancetta and cook until the onion is translucent and the garlic colored, about 10 minutes. Add the tomatoes with all their juices, season with salt and pepper, and cook for another 10 to 15 minutes, stirring from time to time, until soft and mushy.

Add 6 cups of the stock and the drained beans, bring to a boil, and gently boil for 10 minutes. Scoop out ½ cup of soup (without pancetta), purée it or pass it through a food mill, and then return it to the soup.

Add the pasta and cook until al dente, stirring from time to time. The soup should be loose and runny; add more stock as needed, depending on the size of the pasta and how much it absorbs. Stir in the butter and cheese. Taste for seasoning and adjust as needed. Serve in warm bowls.

## Catalan Two-Course Christmas Soup / Escudella i carn d'olla (Catalonia, Spain)

We eat Christmas lunch at my in-laws' house, crowding around the table with my wife's three sisters and their families. But on December 26, those sisters head to the homes of their husbands' families for lunch. With my family in a very distant Washington state, my in-laws now come over to our flat for traditional Christmas soup. Chunky, slightly elbow-shaped pasta shells called *galets de Nadal* are boiled in a broth made from three different kinds of meats (including a football-shaped meatball known as a *pilota*, "ball"), vegetables, and chickpeas. The soup is ladled into bowls and that "stuff" that made the broth so rich is set on platters in the middle of the table to eat as a second course.

To keep large galets (roughly 1 ½ inches long and equally as fat at their widest point) from soaking up *all* of the broth, boil them first in water for 7 minutes and, after quickly draining, finish them for 10 minutes or so in the broth. If using shells smaller than galets, skip this step and add them directly to the broth

| | |  | | |
|--|--|--|--|--|
| ¼ | large chicken (1 to 1 ½ pounds), skin and fat removed | | 1 | parsnip, halved |
| 1 | pound veal, in a single piece | | 5 | quarts water |
| 1 | two-to-three-inch piece veal bone with marrow (about 8 ounces) | | | Salt |
| 1 | small ham hock | | 2 | large eggs |
| ½ | pig's foot (optional) | | 6 | ounces lean ground veal or beef |
| 1 | cup dried chickpeas (about 7 ounces), soaked overnight and rinsed | | 6 | ounces ground pork or unsweetened fresh pork sausage, pulled from the casing |
| ¼ | head green cabbage | | | Freshly ground pepper |
| 2 | carrots, halved crosswise | | ½ | cup breadcrumbs |
| 2 | stalks celery, folded in half | | 12 | ounces galets de Nadal or large pasta snail shells such as lumache rigate |
| 1 | medium onion, peeled and halved | | | |

In a large stockpot over high heat, add the chicken, veal, bone, ham hock, pig's foot (if using), chickpeas, cabbage, carrots, celery, onion, and parsnip and cover with the water. Bring to a boil, and season with 1 ¹/₂ teaspoons of salt. Skim off any foam that comes up to the surface. Lower the heat, cover, and simmer for 3 hours.

While the broth cooks, make the pilota. In a large bowl, beat the eggs, mix in the ground beef and pork,

season with salt and pepper, and mix in the breadcrumbs. Divide the mix in half and form two elongated balls (the pilotes).

After the broth has simmered for 3 hours, remove enough vegetables from the pot so that the pilotes will fit without the soup overflowing. Slide the pilotes into the liquid and simmer for 30 minutes.

In a pasta pot, bring 4 quarts of water to a boil and add 4 teaspoons of salt. When the water returns to a rolling boil, add the pasta. Cook, stirring from time to time to keep the pasta from clumping together, for 7 minutes.

Meanwhile, strain the broth into a large pot, discarding the bones and herbs. Bring the broth to a boil.

Drain the pasta, but do not rinse, shaking off any water that clings to the pasta. Transfer immediately to the broth. Boil for another 10 minutes or until al dente.

While the pasta cooks, transfer the meats, pilotes, and chickpeas to a large serving platter. Cover to keep warm.

Serve the soup as a first course and the meats, pilotes, and chickpeas as a second.

# Tortellini in Capon Broth / Tortellini in brodo di cappone (Bologna, Italy)

The recipe for this Northern Italian Christmas lunch specialty comes from Eleonora Monti Gillen, an Italian friend who not long ago moved to Catalonia from a village in Bologna. (To be more precise, the recipe is from Eleonora's great-grandmother.) Each Christmas, Eleonora sits around the family kitchen table with her mother, brother, grand-mother, and plenty of aunts as they prepare hundreds and hundreds of tortellini—lots of work, but a festive tradition. Five of us spent the better part of a recent winter day around Eleonora's table doing the same. Christmas may have passed, but it still felt festive.

Calculate about fifty tortellini per person. Because the tortellini are cooked and eaten in broth, they are not dusted in flour after folding into shapes.

FOR THE BRODO (BROTH):

| | | | | |
|---|---|---|---|---|
| 1 | whole capon (4 to 7 pounds) or large hen (4 to 6 pounds), cleaned and quartered | | 2 | cherry tomatoes |
| 1 | medium onion, peeled | | 2 | stalks fresh flat-leaf parsley |
| 1 | carrot, scrubbed | | | Salt |
| 1 | celery stalk including leaves, chopped | | 8 | quarts water |

FOR THE PASTA DOUGH:

| | | | | |
|---|---|---|---|---|
| 1 | pound 2 ounces tipo "oo" flour or American unbleached all-purpose flour, plus more for dusting | | 5 | large eggs, at room temperature |

FOR THE FILLING:

| | | | | |
|---|---|---|---|---|
| 6 | ounces ground raw prosciutto | | 1 | whole nutmeg, freshly grated |
| 6 | ounces ground mortadella | | | Salt and freshly ground pepper |
| 6 | ounces ground pork loin | | 2 | large eggs, at room temperature |
| 6 | ounces freshly grated Parmigiano-Reggiano | | | |
| | Parmigiano-Reggiano for grating over | | | |

Prepare the *brodo*: In a stockpot or another large pot over high heat, add the capon, onion, carrot, celery, tomatoes, parsley, and a pinch of salt. Cover with the water, bring to a boil, then reduce the heat to low, cover, and cook at a gentle boil for 2 hours. Strain the stock, reserving the capon meat for another use. (If desired, chill the broth and remove some of the fat that floats to the top.)

Prepare the dough: Use the quantities listed here, and follow the directions for Fresh Egg Pasta on page 101.

Prepare the filling: In a large bowl, mix together the prosciutto, mortadella, pork, Parmigiano-Reggiano, and nutmeg; season with salt and pepper. In another large bowl, beat the eggs and then add the filling, working into a consistent paste.

Divide the pasta into 10 even parts, covering with plastic until ready to use. Divide the filling into ten even parts.

Roll out one piece of the pasta to the thinnest setting in a pasta machine or by hand following the directions on page 101. The final sheet should be 5 inches wide by about 24 to 30 inches long. Lay on a clean cotton sheet folded in half or kitchen towels. With a pasta cutter, cut the pasta lengthwise into 4 even strips (roughly $1^1/4$ inches wide) and then cut crosswise to make squares. In the middle of each square, place about $1/8$ teaspoon of filling.

Taking one square between the fingers, fold it into a triangle, gently pinching down the edges. With the longest side of the triangle facing down, crimp flat the two bottom points and then bring them together around a pinky to form a ring. The two ends should slightly overlap; pinch them together. Now bend over the remaining top corner. Place on the sheet. Repeat with the rest of the squares, laying them out on the towel without touching.

Roll out another piece of dough and repeat until all of the dough and filling is used up. Cover the tortellini in plastic wrap and refrigerate if not used within an hour.

To cook, bring $6^1/2$ quarts of the capon stock to a boil in a clean pot. Add the tortellini, partly cover, and simmer until tender, 8 to 10 minutes. Carefully stir during the first 5 minutes of cooking to keep the tortellini from sticking together. Taste for seasoning and adjust as needed. Remove from the heat, cover, and let the tortellini sit in the broth and absorb more moisture for 10 minutes.

Divide evenly among warm bowls and grate Parmigiano-Reggiano over the top before serving very hot.

# Neretva-Style Eel and Frog Brodet / Neretvanski brodet od jeguje i žabe
(Neretva River Valley, Dalmatia, Croatia)

The rugged coast of Dalmatia opens up into a fertile valley where the Neretva River flows into the Mediterranean Sea. This river valley supplies most of Dubrovnik's (Croatia) agriculture, while the river estuary offers eel and frogs, two important local ingredients. One of the most popular dishes along the coast is seafood *brodet*—a stew cooked in a pot that is shaken, never stirred—but in the Neretva valley, it's traditionally prepared with eel and frogs. One night in Dubrovnik, Maria Vicelić prepared it for me with eel speared the night before and very fresh frogs. ("How many frogs do you add?" I asked, taking notes on the recipe. "As many as you can catch.") Dill stems, Maria explained, "break the muddy taste of river fish." Carp can be substituted for the eel, but cook it for half of the time. And, as Maria advised, "sprinkle the eggs of the carp into the pot at the very end. Yum!"

| | |
|---|---|
| 3 | tablespoons extra-virgin olive oil |
| 1 | medium onion, finely chopped |
| 1 | small dried hot chile, finely chopped, or ¼ teaspoon red pepper flakes |
| 2 | tablespoons tomato concentrate |
| 2 | cups water |
| 2 | fresh dill stems, soft leaves stripped and discarded, cut into 1-inch-long sections |
| 1 | pound eel, skin scrubbed and cut into 1- to 1½-inch-thick steaks |
| | Salt and freshly ground pepper |
| 8 | pairs frog legs, dressed |
| 14 | ounces fusilli, *eliche*, or another short, twisty pasta |

In a heavy pot or Dutch oven over medium heat, heat the oil. Add the onion and chile and cook until the onion is soft and translucent, about 10 minutes. Stir in the tomato concentrate, add the water and the dill, and bring to a simmer.

Generously season the eel with salt and pepper, lay in the pot, and continue to simmer until half cooked, 15 to 20 minutes, depending on the eel. Shake the pot from time to time; do not stir. Add the frog legs, shaking the pot to settle the legs into the broth, and cook for another 15 to 20 minutes. The sauce should be thickened but loose. To thicken further, remove the eel and frogs with a slotted spoon and transfer to a platter; cover and keep warm. Increase the heat and reduce the sauce to desired consistency. Return the eel and frogs to the pan and remove from the heat.

Meanwhile, in a pasta pot, bring 4 quarts of water to a boil and add 4 teaspoons of salt. When the water returns to a rolling boil, add the pasta. Boil the pasta, stirring from time to time to keep it from clumping together, until al dente. Drain, but do not rinse, shaking off any water that clings to the pasta.

Turn the pasta out into a shallow serving bowl, place the eel and frogs on top, and cover with the sauce.

# Handmade Tagliatelle with Fresh White Truffles / Tagliatelle con tartufo bianco (Piedmont, Italy)

Many gastronomes consider truffles to be the culinary summit. The year 2007 was a dry year, and white truffles, which are more aromatic, rarer, and many times more expensive than black ones, sold in the Alba truffle market for upward of $850 for 100 grams (that's $4,000 a pound!). These precious tubers grow around the roots of certain trees and are found in autumn using specially trained dogs who can detect their smell through feet of soil. Following the dogs are their owners, who carry medieval spades and kid leather pouches, the kind I imagined prospectors once carried when looking for gold.

The first time I accompanied a truffle hunter was in Piedmont, on the estate of the Counts of Brondelli di Brondello, but we didn't have such good luck. (Instead, I headed to a Moncalvo trattoria and enoteca called La Bella Rosin to eat *tartufo bianco* as a *supplemento* shaved over fresh pasta one night and over steak tartare the next.) Last autumn, though, in the Tuscan hills around Montespertoli, I was more successful. When I first joined the elderly, forest-green-clad man, he said, "I don't think the dog will find any with you. But you can walk along." Thirty seconds later, the dog leapt over a shrubby embankment and began frantically digging at the dirt. We followed and dug up a golf ball–size truffle. The dog was rewarded, though not with the truffle it so desperately wanted to devour. That was our reward.

| | | | | |
|---|---|---|---|---|
| 14 | ounces Fresh Egg Pasta (page 101) | | 1 ½ | ounces freshly grated Parmigiano-Reggiano |
| 1 | white truffle | | | Freshly ground pepper |
| | Salt | | | |
| 2 | tablespoons high-quality butter, cut into pieces | | | |

Prepare the pasta and cut into tagliatelle ribbons as directed.

Using a brush, clean the truffle, removing any dirt. Wipe with a damp cloth.

In a pasta pot, bring 4 quarts of water to a boil and add 4 teaspoons of salt. When the water returns to a rolling boil, add the pasta. Cook, stirring from time to time to keep the pasta from clumping together, until al dente, 2 to 5 minutes, depending on the thickness of the pasta. Drain but do not rinse, shaking off any water that clings to the pasta.

Divide the pasta among four warm bowls. Divide the butter and about 1 ounce of the cheese among them. Season with salt and pepper and toss to blend. Shave the truffle in paper-thin slices over top. Serve with the remaining ¹/₂ ounce cheese on the side.

## Primary Source: Carla Meucci, Montespertoli, Tuscany

One recent autumn, my six-year-old daughter, Alba, and I spent a week in a villa set among rolling vineyards near the Tuscan town of Montespertoli. A local cook named Carla Meucci came to the villa one afternoon to give us a master class in preparing fresh pasta. Flamboyant and funny, with a billowing, contagious laugh, red-and-white-checked apron, and towering chef's hat, Carla captured Alba's attention immediately.

Carla organized the kitchen, put a meat ragù on the stove to begin its long simmer, and then set out a large, round board on the kitchen table for the pasta dough. She worked eggs into the mound of powdery-soft flour as well as some cloudy, jade-green olive oil (from the villa's own trees) that gave the dough a lusty sheen. Alba photographed not just every step of the process with a small digital camera but took close-ups of each ingredient and tool involved. After the dough had rested for an hour, Carla rolled it out and then began passing it through her fifty-year-old hand-cranked pasta machine, cutting, finally, long strips of tagliatelle.

By the time the noodles had been boiled and tossed with the ragù, Alba had taken over 150 photos. (She then momentarily forgot about the camera, and devoured three heaped plates of the pasta.)

Back home in Barcelona, Alba made a twenty-page book titled "How To Make Fresh Pasta". Each step has a page with instructions ("add lots of flour"; "knead for a long time") with a photo pasted opposite to illustrate. She took the book to school and showed her first-grade class (justification for her week's absence from class), and then shelved it, appropriately, among my cookbooks.

For King's Day, the following winter, I received the same brand and style of pasta machine as Carla's. Alba took her book off the shelf and together we made pasta, going though the book page by page (though I also snuck peaks at my own notes to see exactly how much was "lots" and how long was "a long time"). We kneaded and rolled and then fed the dough through the machine's rollers; I turned the crank while Alba caught the sheets. As we notched down the rollers, the sheets got progressively thinner, until we cut them into ribbons of tagliatelle. She dusted with them flour and laid them out on towels to dry.

As I put a pot of water on to boil—no need for notes from here on—she carefully put her book away on the shelf, the covers dusted white with tiny fingerprints.

It's Alba's first cookbook—a paean to Carla's fresh pasta—and a worthy first subject if there ever was one.

# Fresh Spinach Pasta with Pine Nuts /
## Pasta d'espinacs amb pinyons (Barcelona, Spain)

The tall pine trees around my in-laws' summer beach apartment drop an endless supply of cones laden with pine nuts. My daughters spend hours shaking the seeds from the cones and cracking them open to expel the delicate, oblong white seeds. But both girls have an insatiable appetite for pine nuts and, unless watched, will deviate from a simple rule once followed by my wife and her sisters when they were young: cracked seeds into the mouth, perfect ones into a jar for use in the kitchen. In our kitchen, we love to use the resinous-tasting wild pine nuts tossed with fresh spinach pasta. It makes a simple and delicious dinner; one we repeat even when the jar is empty and we need to buy them at the market.

FOR THE PASTA DOUGH:

| | | | | |
|---|---|---|---|---|
| 8 | ounces tender spinach leaves, stems trimmed | | 2 | large eggs, at room temperature |
| | Salt | | 1 | tablespoon extra-virgin olive oil |
| 2 | cups tipo "oo" flour or American unbleached all-purpose flour, plus more for dusting | | | |
| | Salt | | 1 ½ | ounces freshly grated Parmigiano-Reggiano |
| ¼ | cup pine nuts | | | Freshly ground pepper |
| 2 | tablespoons butter, cut into pieces | | | |

Prepare the dough: Wash the spinach in at least three changes of water. Drain in a colander. Place in a large pot over medium heat, add a pinch of salt, cover, and cook until wilted and soft, 6 to 8 minutes. Transfer to the colander to drain. Once cool enough to handle, press out any moisture with your hands. Very finely chop.

Prepare the pasta and cut into tagliatelle ribbons as directed on page 101 using the quantities listed here with this addition—whisk the eggs with the spinach and a pinch of salt before incorporating them into the flour.

In a pasta pot, bring 4 quarts of water to a boil and add 4 teaspoons of salt. When the water returns to a rolling boil, add the pasta. Cook, stirring from time to time to keep the pasta from clumping together, until al dente,

2 to 5 minutes, depending on the thickness of the pasta. Drain but do not rinse, shaking off any water that clings to the pasta.

Meanwhile, in a small sauté pan or skillet over low heat, dry roast the pine nuts until golden and fragrant, 6 to 8 minutes. Remove from the heat.

Divide the pasta among four warm bowls. Divide the butter and about 1 ounce of the cheese among them. Season with salt and pepper and toss to blend. Scatter the pine nuts over the top. Serve with the remaining cheese on the side.

# Fresh Nettle Pasta (Malta)

Flipping through Matty Cremona's lovely book *A Year in the Country: Life and Food in Rural Malta* in the library, I came upon a recipe for nettle pasta. I loved the idea, and that spring, visiting friends in the countryside north of Barcelona, we found a patch of nettles while strolling after lunch. The next time we went to visit, we took gloves. Wearing these, and picking only the softest leaves, we quickly filled a shopping bag. Back home, we prepared a lovely green pasta with the nettles much as we would with spinach and dressed it simply following Cremona's suggestion, *aglio e olio* (garlic and olive oil). To this we added, instead of the wild herbs she mentions, some spicy red pepper flakes. Perfect.

If you can't find nettles, substitute fresh spinach leaves (see page 115).

FOR THE PASTA DOUGH:

| | | | |
|---|---|---|---|
| 2 | tightly packed cups tender nettle leaves (about 6 ounces), cleaned and trimmed | 2 | large eggs, at room temperature |
| | Salt | 1 | tablespoon extra-virgin olive oil |
| 2 | cups unbleached all-purpose flour, plus more for dusting | | |

FOR AGLIO E OLIO:

| | | | |
|---|---|---|---|
| ¼ | cup extra-virgin olive oil | 1 ½ | ounces freshly grated ġbejna cheese or Parmigiano-Reggiano |
| 4 | garlic cloves, minced | | Salt and pepper |
| 4 | pinches red pepper flakes | | |

Prepare the dough: Bring a large pot of water to a boil. Wearing gloves, add the nettles and a pinch of salt, boil for 20 minutes, and drain in a colander. The stingers deactivate through cooking, so now the leaves can be handled freely. Once cool enough to handle, press out any moisture with your hands. Very finely chop.

Prepare the pasta and cut into tagliatelle ribbons as directed on page 101 using the quantities listed here with this addition—whisk the eggs with the nettles and a pinch of salt before incorporating them into the flour.

In a pasta pot, bring 4 quarts of water to a boil and add 4 teaspoons of salt. When the water returns to a rolling boil, add the pasta. Cook, stirring from time to time to keep the pasta from clumping together, until al dente, 2 to 5 minutes, depending on the thickness of the pasta. Drain but do not rinse, shaking off any water that clings to the pasta.

Meanwhile, prepare the aglio e olio sauce: In a small sauté pan or skillet over medium-low heat, heat the oil and add the garlic. When the garlic begins to turn golden, add the red pepper flakes and remove the pan from the heat. Do not let the garlic burn.

Toss the aglio e olio with the pasta. Divide the pasta among four warm bowls. Divide about 1 ounce of the cheese among them and season with salt and pepper. Serve with the remaining cheese on the side.

# Fresh Algerian Noodles with Chicken / Rechta au poulet (Algeria)

Algeria boasts a number of delicious "indigenous" pastas, usually triple steamed in a couscoussier before being tossed with sauce. My favorite is *rechta*, fresh pasta made with hard durum wheat semolina flour and water, rolled out into fine sheets, and cut into very thin noodles. During steaming and tossing, they break up into 3- to 4-inch-long pieces. The sauce here is simple—chicken and turnips—but with warm flavors completely in harmony with the taste of the pasta.

This dish can be prepared by boiling dried vermicelli or tagliarini noodles broken into 3- or 4-inch-lengths.

FOR THE PASTA DOUGH:

| | |
|---|---|
| 2 | cups fine durum wheat semolina flour (about 12 ounces) |
| | Salt |
| ¾ | cup water |
| | Cornstarch for dusting |
| 1 | tablespoon extra-virgin olive oil |

FOR THE SAUCE:

| | |
|---|---|
| ½ | large chicken, cleaned and cut into 4 pieces, or 2 pounds bone-in chicken legs and thighs |
| 1 | medium onion, grated |
| 1 | tablespoon olive oil |
| 2 | tablespoons butter or smen |
| 4 | turnips, scrubbed and quartered lengthwise |
| | Salt and freshly ground pepper |
| 6 | cups water |
| | Ground cinnamon for dusting |

Prepare the dough: Place the flour in a large bowl, add a pinch of salt, and begin working in the water little by little until forming a consistent ball. (There might be a bit of leftover water.) On a clean surface, knead until supple and elastic. Cover with plastic wrap and let rest for 30 minutes.

Break off one-third or one-fourth of the dough; rewrap the rest in plastic until ready to use.

Roll out one piece of the pasta to the thinnest setting in a pasta machine or by hand following the directions on page 101. Cut the sheets into very fine strands. Dust with cornstarch to keep from sticking. Let dry on a cornstarch-dusted towel for 15 minutes. Cover with a towel until ready to steam. Repeat with the remaining dough.

Meanwhile, begin preparing the sauce: In the bottom of a couscoussier or in a large pot, add the chicken, onion, and olive oil. Swirl to coat, and cook over medium heat until the chicken is browned and the onion begins to soften, about 5 minutes. Add the turnips, season with salt and pepper, and cover with the water. Then bring to a boil, lower the heat, cover, and simmer for 50 minutes.

Meanwhile, shake the excess cornstarch from the pasta and work in the olive oil with your hands to keep pasta from sticking together.

While the stew cooks, steam the rechta following the directions on page 99. Steam for 5 minutes, beginning the counting once the steam rises up through the noodles.

Transfer to a wide platter, sprinkle with cool water, and separate any noodles that are stuck together. Let rest for 5 minutes. Return to the top of the couscoussier and steam for 5 more minutes, again beginning the counting once the steam rises up through the noodles. Return to the platter, sprinkle with water, and separate noodles that are stuck together. Let rest for 5 minutes. Return to the couscoussier for a third time and steam for 5 minutes or until tender.

Place the noodles in a wide serving bowl and toss with the butter. Moisten with some broth, lightly dust with cinnamon, and top with the pieces of chicken and turnips. Serve the remaining broth on the side.

# Busiate with Trapani Pesto of Tomatoes, Garlic, Basil, and Almonds / Busiate al pesto trapanese (Trapani, Sicily)

This memorable pesto from the city of Trapani on Sicily's west coast uses almonds instead of pine nuts and blends in ripe, fresh tomatoes. One lovely spring, as wild flowers carpeted this entire part of the island, my wife and I devoured this dish made with small cherry tomatoes bursting with juice and sweet flavor. Superb.

| | | | | |
|---|---|---|---|---|
| 1 ½ | ounces toasted almonds, skins slipped off | | Salt | |
| 1 | garlic clove, peeled | | 2 | ounces freshly grated pecorino cheese |
| 8 | fresh basil leaves, finely shredded | | 1 | pound ripe cherry tomatoes |
| 4 | tablespoons extra-virgin olive oil | | 10 | ounces busiate, *fusilli lunghi*, or bucatini |

In a mortar, pound the almonds, garlic, basil, ½ tablespoon of the oil, and a pinch of salt with a pestle into a gritty paste; or quickly blend them in a food processor. Mix in the remaining 3 ½ tablespoons of oil. Transfer to a large bowl and stir in half of the cheese.

Without losing any of the juices, quarter half of the tomatoes and add to the bowl; gently crush with the back of a fork. Halve the remaining tomatoes and add to the bowl. Mix well and set aside to allow the flavors to meld while preparing the pasta.

In a pasta pot, bring 4 quarts of water to a boil and add 4 teaspoons of salt. When the water returns to a rolling boil, add the pasta. Boil the pasta, stirring from time to time to keep it from clumping together, until al dente. Drain but do not rinse, shaking off any water that clings to the pasta.

Return the pasta to the pot. Over very low heat, gradually add the pesto mixture, tossing until thoroughly mixed.

Serve in warm bowls with the remaining cheese on the side.

# Conchiglie with Lobster and Broccoli / Conchiglie con aragosta e broccoli (Sardinia, Italy)

The northwestern Sardinian port city of Alghero was a Catalan (then Spanish) outpost for 350 years, until 1720. So no wonder, then, that the most famous way to prepare Alghero's celebrated lobsters is *alla catalana*, with onions and tomatoes. Tasty. But I love how Benito Carbonella, the owner and chef at Al Tuguri restaurant, pairs them with broccoli and then tosses them with *conchiglie*. With its spectacular colors and even more spectacular flavors, this recipe, adapted from Carbonella's, is a particular favorite of ours to serve to guests at home.

| | |
|---|---|
| 1 | live female lobster (1 to 1 ½ pounds) |
| 1 | pound broccoli, stems trimmed and broken into bite-size florets |
| | Salt |
| 14 | ounces conchiglie |
| 6 | tablespoons extra-virgin olive oil |
| 2 | garlic cloves, minced |

| | |
|---|---|
| | Peperoncino or red pepper flakes |
| 2 | teaspoons brandy |
| 1 ½ | tablespoons dry white wine |
| 1 ½ | tablespoons white wine vinegar |
| 1 | tablespoon finely chopped fresh flat-leaf parsley |
| | Freshly ground pepper |

With a very sharp knife, split the live lobster in half lengthwise, cutting along the belly and catching any juice that falls. Reserve the eggs and liver. Discard the head and trim the feet. Cut the body into cube-shaped pieces, keeping the meat attached to the shell if possible. Pick out any tiny shards of shell. Gently crack the large claws so that they remain intact but the meat will be easily accessible when eating.

Steam the broccoli until done but still firm. Remove from the heat and cover to keep warm.

In a pasta pot, bring 4 quarts of water to a boil and add 4 teaspoons of salt. When the water returns to a rolling boil, add the pasta. Boil the pasta, stirring from time to time to keep it from clumping together, until al dente.

Meanwhile, in a large sauté pan or skillet over medium heat, heat the oil. Add the garlic, a generous pinch of peperoncino, and the lobster cubes. As soon as the lobster changes color from pearly white to plain white, about 2 minutes, add the reserved lobster eggs, lobster liquid, and the brandy. Stir and immediately add the wine and vinegar. Cook, stirring occasionally, for 2 minutes. Add the reserved broccoli and a pinch of salt, stir gently, and cover, allowing the flavors to meld for 3 to 4 minutes. Splash in a bit of water, if needed, to keep it moist.

Drain the pasta but do not rinse, shaking off any water that clings to it. Toss it with the lobster and broccoli. Serve in warm bowls, sprinkling parsley and a generous amount of pepper over the top.

## Linguine with Santa Lucia-Style Octopus / Linguine alla luciana (Naples, Italy)

Fishermen's dishes tend to be straightforward and, even though they often include only a few ingredients, bursting with flavor. This octopus dish, named after the old fishermen's quarter in Naples, Santa Lucia, is no exception. It can be eaten as is, but is delicious served over long, thin pasta. This recipe is adapted from Francesca Marigliano, the mother of an artist friend in Naples named Vincenzo Giugliano.

| | | | | |
|---|---|---|---|---|
| 2 | pounds small fresh octopus | | ½ | cup white wine |
| 3 | tablespoons extra-virgin olive oil | | | Salt |
| 2 | garlic cloves, minced | | 14 | ounces linguine or vermicelli |
| 1 | pound plum tomatoes, peeled, seeded, and finely chopped | | 2 | tablespoons finely chopped fresh flat-leaf parsley |

Clean the octopus. Remove and discard the mouth, eyes, and ink sack. Rinse under running water. Cut into pieces just larger than bite size.

In a large, heavy sauté pan or skillet over medium-high heat, heat the oil. Add the octopus and cook until the octopus has released all of its water, about 10 minutes. Add the garlic and tomatoes, reduce the heat to low, cover, and cook, stirring occasionally, for 40 minutes. Add some warm water if the sauce looks about to dry out.

Stir in the wine, and cook uncovered, stirring occasionally, for 10 minutes. The sauce should be rich, deep red, and slightly runny.

Meanwhile, in a pasta pot, bring 4 quarts of water to a boil and add 4 teaspoons of salt. When the water returns to a rolling boil, add the pasta. Cook, stirring from time to time to keep the pasta from clumping together, until al dente. Drain but do not rinse, shaking off any water that clings to the pasta.

Toss the pasta with the sauce and serve in warm bowls, generously sprinkled with the parsley.

# Bucatini with Sardines and Fennel / Pasta con le sarde (Sicily, Italy)

Sicily's most famous dish is an exuberant showcase of local ingredients, a resplendent symphony from the hills and sea—wild fennel, fresh sardines, a couple of salted anchovies, sweet raisins and earthy pine nuts, saffron . . . A tone-perfect combination of sweet and savory.

| | | | | |
|---|---|---|---|---|
| 1 | pound fresh fennel greens, preferably wild, washed (see Note) | | 3 | tablespoons extra-virgin olive oil |
| | Salt | | 2 | medium onions, finely chopped |
| 2 | ounces raisins | | 4 | anchovy fillets, rinsed and patted dry |
| 10 | strands saffron, dry roasted | | | Freshly ground pepper |
| ¼ | cup warm water | | 2 | ounces pine nuts |
| 8 | fresh whole sardines | | 14 | ounces bucatini or *perciatelli* |

Bring 4 ½ quarts of water to a boil in a pasta pot. Add the fennel and 2 hearty pinches of salt and boil until tender, about 10 minutes. Transfer with a slotted spoon to a platter to cool. Remove the pot from heat, cover, and reserve the water.

Once the fennel is cool enough to handle, finely chop. Soak the raisins in tepid water for 15 minutes; drain. Soak the saffron in the ¹/₄ cup of warm water; reserve.

Gently scale the sardines with a knife, then fillet them; hold a sardine with one hand and with the other rock the head first upward breaking the neck, then downward, and finally firmly pulling it away to draw out the entrails. Run a finger through the cavity to make sure it is clean. At the base of the tail, make an angled incision to the bone using a sharp knife. Slide a thumbnail under the fillet and gently pull it away from the spine. Repeat on other side. Check closely for any bones. Rinse and pat dry with paper towels.

In a large sauté pan or skillet over medium heat, heat the oil. Add the onions and cook until they begin to soften, about 5 minutes. Add the anchovies and cook, stirring frequently, until the onions are golden and the anchovies have dissolved, about 5 more minutes. Add the reserved fennel greens, season with salt and pepper, and cook, stirring occasionally, for 5 minutes. Stir in the raisins and pine nuts and cook for 5 more minutes. Add the sardines, and cook for a final 5 minutes, stirring occasionally to break up the fillets. Moisten with the saffron-infused water and remove from the heat.

Meanwhile, return the reserved fennel greens water in the pasta pot to a boil. Add 2 teaspoons of salt. When the water returns to a rolling boil, add the pasta. Boil the pasta, stirring from time to time to keep it from clumping together, until al dente. Drain but do not rinse, shaking off any water that clings to the pasta.

Toss the pasta with the sauce and serve in warm bowls.

NOTE: SUBSTITUTE THE FENNEL GREENS WITH ¹/₂ FENNEL BULB AND ITS FRONDS (ABOUT ¹/₂ POUND). CUT INTO TWO OR THREE PIECES AND BOIL UNTIL TENDER, ABOUT 20 MINUTES. FINELY CHOP.

## Pappardelle with Duck Ragù / Pappardelle con l'anatra (Florence, Italy)

One autumn, recently, near Montespertoli in western Tuscany, I was nosing around the kitchen of the villa where I was staying and found on a high shelf, covered in spiderwebs and dust, a gem of a Florentine cookbook, Paolo Petroni's 1974 *Il libro della vera cucina fiorentina*. Among the many country-style recipes was one for duck ragù, which I have adapted here. Duck season hadn't yet begun—hunters and dogs were walking the fields around the villa for *fagiano* (pheasant) and *lepre* (hare)—but it would soon.

| | | | | |
|---|---|---|---|---|
| 14 | ounces fresh or dried pappardelle | | 2 | ounces cured pancetta, chopped |
| ½ | small cleaned duck, liver and heart reserved | | 1 | cup white wine |
| ¼ | cup extra-virgin olive oil | | 1 | pound tomatoes, peeled, seeded, and finely chopped, juices reserved |
| 1 | medium onion, finely chopped | | | Salt and freshly ground pepper |
| ½ | carrot, finely chopped | | | Fennel seeds |
| ½ | stalk celery with leaves, finely chopped | | 1½ | ounces freshly grated Parmigiano-Reggiano |
| 1 | garlic clove, minced | | | |
| 1 | heaping tablespoon finely chopped fresh flat-leaf parsley | | | |

If preparing fresh pappardelle, follow the directions on page 101, cutting the pasta into 3/4- to 1-inch-wide ribbons.

Cut the duck into 3 or 4 large pieces, remove the skin, and trim any excess fat. Rinse under running water. Mince half of the liver and the heart and set aside until the end of the dish. (Discard the remaining liver and heart.)

Prepare a sofrito. In a large, heavy sauté pan or skillet over medium heat, heat the oil. Add the onion and cook until it begins to soften, about 5 minutes. Add the carrot, celery, garlic, parsley, and pancetta, and cook until the onion is translucent and the garlic colored, about 10 minutes. Increase the heat slightly to medium-high, add the duck, and cook, turning the pieces over frequently, until they have browned, about 5 minutes.

Stir in the wine and cook until it has completely evaporated. Add the tomatoes and all their juices and season with salt and pepper. Then reduce the heat to low, cover, and cook, stirring occasionally, for 1 hour. Add a few tablespoons of warm water if the sauce looks about to dry out.

Remove the pieces of duck from the pan and debone when cool enough to handle. Tear the meat into bite-size pieces and return them to the sauce along with the minced liver and heart. Sprinkle in a pinch of the fennel seeds. Cook for a final 2 to 3 minutes allowing the fennel to perfume the sauce.

Meanwhile, in a pasta pot, bring 4 quarts of water to a boil and add 4 teaspoons of salt. When the water returns to a rolling boil, add the pasta. Cook, stirring from time to time to keep the pasta from clumping together, until al dente. Drain but do not rinse, shaking off any water that clings to the pasta.

Toss the pasta with the sauce and serve in warm bowls, generously sprinkled with the cheese.

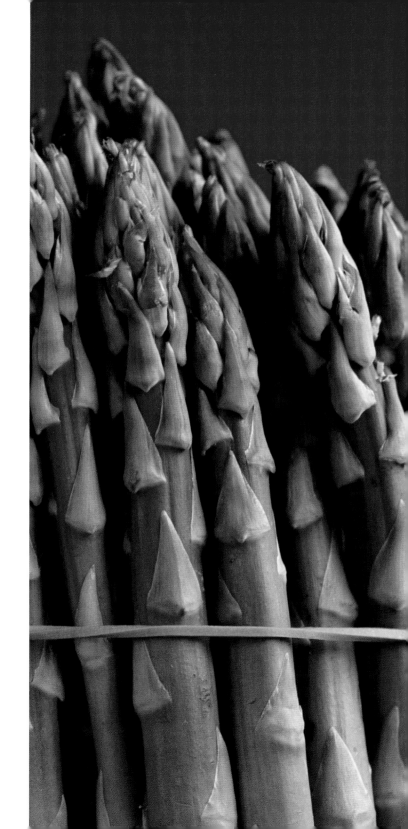

# Pasta with Eggplant, Tomatoes, and Basil /
## Pasta alla Norma (Catania, Sicily, Italy)

This dish, from the city of Catania, at the foot of Mount Etna on the eastern coast of Sicily, is named after the opera of the city's most famous son, composer Vincenzo Bellini. *Norma* was first produced at Teatro alla Scala in Milan in 1831 and is a classic in the lavish tradition of *bel canto*, "beautiful singing." A fitting name, then, for this fantastic mélange of flavors.

| | | | | |
|---|---|---|---|---|
| 1 | pound eggplant | | | Freshly ground black pepper |
| | Salt | | 10 | fresh basil leaves, shredded |
| ¼ | cup extra-virgin olive oil | | | Oil for frying |
| 1 | medium onion, finely chopped | | 14 | ounces spaghetti or penne rigate |
| 2 | garlic cloves, minced | | 1 ½ | ounces freshly grated ricotta salata |
| 1 | pound tomatoes, peeled, seeded, and finely chopped | | | |

Wash the eggplant and cut into 1-inch-square cubes. Liberally salt and place in a colander to drain for 30 minutes. Rinse thoroughly with cool running water and gently squeeze out some of the excess liquid. Pat dry with paper towels.

Meanwhile, prepare a sofrito. In a large, heavy saucepan over medium-low heat, heat the olive oil. Add the onion and cook until it begins to soften, about 5 minutes. Add the garlic and cook until the onion is translucent and the garlic colored but not burned, about 5 more minutes. Add the tomatoes, season with salt and pepper, and cook for another 15 to 20 minutes, stirring from time to time and breaking up any pieces of tomatoes, until mushy and darkened. Add half of the basil. Stir in a few tablespoons of water to loosen the sauce, if needed.

Meanwhile, fry the eggplant. Heat about 1 inch deep of the frying oil over high heat to smoking in a large sauté pan or skillet. Working in batches, fry the pieces until golden on the outside and tender on the inside when poked with the tip of a sharp knife. Remove with a slotted spoon and lay on a paper towel–lined plate to drain.

Meanwhile, in a pasta pot, bring 4 quarts of water to a boil and add 4 teaspoons of salt. When the water returns to a rolling boil, add the pasta. Cook, stirring from time to time to keep the pasta from clumping together, until al dente. Drain but do not rinse, shaking off any water that clings to the pasta.

Toss the pasta with the sauce. Divide among four warm bowls. Top with the cheese, the eggplant, and then the remaining basil.

# Fusilli in Cream Sauce with Sausage and Fennel Seeds / Fusilli all'abruzzese (Abruzzo, Italy)

This quick dish comes from the Abruzzo region east of Rome, the center of Italy's dried pasta industry. It's creamy, almost sweet, and delightfully aromatized with fennel seeds, which are added only for the last few minutes of cooking.

| | | | | |
|---|---|---|---|---|
| 2 | tablespoons extra-virgin olive oil | | 1 | cup heavy cream |
| 1 | medium onion, finely chopped | | ¼ | teaspoon fennel seeds |
| | Salt | | | Freshly ground pepper |
| 12 | ounces fresh unsweetened pork sausages, pulled from the casing, and pinched into marble-size pieces | | 14 | ounces fusilli |

In a large, heavy sauté pan or skillet over medium heat, heat the oil. Add the onion and a pinch of salt and cook, stirring frequently, until the onion is soft and translucent, about 10 minutes. Add the sausage and cook until the sausage is cooked through, about 5 minutes. Add the cream, fennel seeds, and pepper, increase the heat to high, and cook until the cream has thickened slightly, 5 to 10 minutes.

Meanwhile, in a pasta pot, bring 4 quarts of water to a boil and add 4 teaspoons of salt. When the water returns to a rolling boil, add the pasta. Cook, stirring from time to time to keep the pasta from clumping together, until al dente. Drain but do not rinse, shaking off any water that clings to the pasta.

Toss the pasta with the sauce and serve in warm bowls, liberally dusted with freshly ground pepper.

# Cheese-Filled Ravioli with Garlicky Breadcrumbs (Spain)

Stuffed pasta comes in about every shape—from half-moons to small squares the size of postage stamps—and filled with about every ingredient (pumpkin is a favorite of ours; so are wild mushrooms). But sometimes, it's just basic, cheese-filled pasta that I crave the most. Usually we toss it in good olive oil and some Parmigiano-Reggiano, but some days we like to sprinkle garlicky, butter-fried breadcrumbs over the top for a change in texture. Breadsticks work great for this. One ounce of breadsticks ground in a blender equals a generous ¼ cup of crunchy crumbs.

| | | | |
|---|---|---|---|
| 14 | ounces Fresh Egg Pasta (page 101) | | |

FOR THE FILLING:

| | | | |
|---|---|---|---|
| 1 | large egg, at room temperature | ¼ | cup freshly grated Parmigiano-Reggiano |
| 1 | cup ricotta | | Salt and freshly ground pepper |

FOR THE TOPPING:

| | | | |
|---|---|---|---|
| 3 | tablespoons butter | ¼ | coarse breadcrumbs |
| 1 | garlic clove, minced | | |
| | Salt | | Extra-virgin olive oil |

Prepare the Fresh Egg Pasta as directed.

Prepare the filling: In a medium bowl, beat the egg. Add the ricotta and Parmigiano-Reggiano, season with salt and pepper, and mix to an even consistency.

Working with about a quarter of the pasta dough at a time, roll out the dough into sheets. Lay out on a floured dish towel. Dollop a tablespoon of filling every 2 inches or so along one side. Lightly brush the edges and between the dollops of filling with a touch of water. Fold the pasta over in half lengthwise. Working away from the fold, smooth out any trapped air bubbles and seal by gently pressing down on the edges. With a serrated ravioli or pizza cutter, cut the pasta into 2-inch squares. Crimp the edges with the fingers if needed. Lay out the ravioli pieces on a floured kitchen towel; do not allow them to touch each other. Dust with flour and cover with a clean kitchen towel until ready to use.

Roll out another piece of dough and repeat until all of the dough and filling is used. Cover the ravioli in plastic wrap and refrigerate if not used within an hour.

Prepare the topping: In a small sauté pan or skillet over medium-low heat, melt the butter, add the garlic and cook until it is fragrant and begins to turn golden, about 2 minutes. Sprinkle in the breadcrumbs and fry until golden without allowing the garlic to burn.

Meanwhile, in a pasta pot, bring 4 quarts of water to a boil and add 4 teaspoons of salt. When the water returns to a simmer, add the pasta. Cook, stirring from time to time to keep the pasta from clumping together, until al dente. Drain but do not rinse, shaking off any water that clings to the pasta.

Gently toss the pasta with olive oil. Divide among four warm bowls and sprinkle with the breadcrumbs.

## Dalmatian Pasticada / Dalmatinska pašticada (Dalmatia, Croatia)

The celebrated Corfu dish of stewed veal and tomato sauce spiced with cinnamon, cloves, and nutmeg known as *pastitsada* is a legacy of the Venetian rule that lasted from 1401 until 1797. The Venetians also ruled Dalmatia (the middle and southern section of Croatia's coast) for roughly that same time period and left a similarly named, just as loved, but not identical meat-and-tomato dish. In Croatia, the veal is marinated in vinegar and wine and then slowly braised in the marinade along with prunes, smoke-cured pancetta, and herbs. The best I've eaten was at a rustic *konoba* (tavern) in Split called Varoš—dark, large tables, an open kitchen with wood-fired grill, generous portions— where the meat was cooked to succulent perfection in a plush, smoky-sweet tomato sauce laced with both red wine and a local sweet tawny dessert wine called Prošek. Perfect for that blustery winter night.

| | |
|---|---|
| 3 | pounds beef round roast, in a single piece, tied with cotton kitchen string to keep its shape |
| ¾ | cup red wine |
| ¾ | cup Prošek or sweet sherry |
| ¼ | cup red wine vinegar |
| 2 | medium onions, finely chopped |
| 4 | garlic cloves, minced |
| 2 | bay leaves |
| ½ | teaspoon freshly ground nutmeg |
| | Salt and freshly ground pepper |
| 3 | tablespoons extra-virgin olive oil |
| 1 | fourteen-ounce can peeled Italian tomatoes, finely chopped, juices reserved |
| 1½ | ounces smoked pancetta or bacon, finely chopped |
| 20 | prunes, pitted |
| 20 | ounces orecchiette or another short pasta |

The day before serving, marinate the meat. In a medium bowl, mix together the wine, Prošek, vinegar, onions, garlic, bay leaves, and nutmeg and season with salt and pepper. Place the meat in a nonreactive container, ideally just longer and wider than the roast, and cover with the marinade. Turn the meat over to coat with the marinade, then cover and refrigerate. Marinate for 24 hours, turning the meat from time to time. Remove the meat and drain, reserving the marinade.

In a Dutch oven or heavy sauté pan or skillet over high heat, heat the oil. Add the meat and brown, turning frequently, about 5 minutes. Lower the heat, pour in the marinade with the onions, garlic, and bay leaves, and add the tomatoes with their reserved juices, pancetta, and prunes. Cook over low heat at a gentle simmer for 1½ hours, turning the meat occasionally.

Remove the meat from the pan. Cut into thin slices. Remove the bay leaves from the sauce. Transfer 6 of the prunes from the sauce to a plate. Purée the rest of the sauce in a blender or pass it through a food mill. Stir in some water to keep it loose, if needed.

Return the meat slices and 6 prunes to the pan and cover with the puréed sauce. Cook over low heat for 10 minutes. Add in more water as needed to keep the sauce loose; the final consistency should be like a medium gravy.

Meanwhile, in a pasta pot, bring 4 quarts of water to a boil and add 4 teaspoons of salt. When the water returns to a rolling boil, add the pasta. Boil the pasta, stirring from time to time to keep it from clumping together, until al dente. Drain but do not rinse, shaking off any water that clings to the pasta.

Turn the pasta out onto a long serving dish. Lay the meat slices along one side and cover with the sauce.

Serve the meat slices layered on plates alongside pasta with the sauce spooned over top.

## Pinotxo's Fideos with Pork Ribs and Fresh Sausage /
## Fideos con costillas de cerdo y salchichas (Barcelona, Spain)

Bar Pinotxo, just inside the entrance of Barcelona's La Boqueria market (see page 136), offers *cuina de mercat*, or "market cooking," at its best. The dishes offer fresh ingredients, bold flavors, and straightforward cooking techniques—though there is usually an unexpected, but perfectly placed, ingredient or two. Here, anchovy and sweet red *choricero* pepper make sly appearances. This recipe is adapted from Pinotxo's own eponymous book that they (at last!) published a few years back.

| | | | |
|---|---|---|---|
| 2 | garlic cloves, peeled | 4 | Spanish onions, finely chopped |
| 1 | tablespoon finely chopped fresh flat-leaf parsley | 1 | tablespoon conserved *choricero* pepper paste (see Note) |
| 1 | anchovy fillet | 1 | tablespoon tomato concentrate |
| ½ | pound pork ribs, cut into ¾- to 1-inch pieces | 8 | ounces medium-thick (Number 2) fideos |
| | Salt and freshly ground pepper | 4 | cups Chicken Stock (page 33) |
| 3 | tablespoons extra-virgin olive oil | | |
| ½ | pound unsweetened fresh pork sausage links, pulled from the casing and pinched into marble-size pieces | | |

Prepare the picada. In a mortar, pound 1 of the garlic cloves, the parsley, and the anchovy with a pestle into a gritty paste, loosened with 1 or 2 tablespoons of water as necessary. (You can also quickly blend them in a food processor with 1 or 2 tablespoons of water.)

Season the ribs with salt and pepper.

Prepare a sofrito. In a large, ovenproof cazuela or heavy sauté pan or skillet over medium-low heat, heat the oil. Add the sausage, ribs, and remaining garlic clove and cook until the meat is browned, about 5 minutes. Add the onions and cook, stirring occasionally, until the onions are soft and golden, about 10 minutes. Stir in the *choricero* paste, tomato concentrate, and the picada. Swirl 2 tablespoons of water around the mortar to clean it out; add that liquid to the pan. Cook, stirring frequently, for 10 minutes, adding in a few tablespoons of warm water if the sofrito looks about to dry out.

Preheat the broiler and set the oven rack in the center of the oven.

Add the fideos to the sofrito and stir until thoroughly coated.

Slide the cazuela into the oven and broil until the fideos begin to color, about 10 minutes. The tips of the fideos can be dark brown but do not let them blacken.

Meanwhile, warm the stock.

When the fideos are browned, return the cazuela to the stove. Pour in the stock and bring to a boil over high heat. Reduce the heat to medium-low and cook until the fideos are al dente. Taste for seasoning and adjust as needed. Remove from the heat and let rest for 5 minutes before serving.

NOTE: SUBSTITUTE THE CHORICERO PASTE WITH 1 TABLESPOON OF SWEET PIMENTÓN (PAPRIKA) DISSOLVED IN JUST ENOUGH WATER TO FORM A PASTE.

Tucked just inside the La Boqueria, the cavernous food market halfway down Barcelona's Las Ramblas, is Pinotxo, a narrow bar offering traditional, seasonal Catalan *cuina de mercat*, or "market cooking," at its finest.

I like to come for a substantial breakfast ("with fork and knife," as the Catalans say), and usually order stewed chickpeas with blood sausage, pine nuts, and raisins. Some days I get baby squid flash-fried with tiny white beans or, in winter, when a cold wind is blowing through the market, one of their other specialties, *cap i pota*, a rich stew made from the head and feet of veal. Famous Juanito greets everyone and pours glasses of cava and makes *tallats* (espresso with a shot of warm milk) while his two nephews, Albert and Jordi, do the cooking. Watching them work is the best education in town.

There has nearly always been an open-air market on approximately this site. Las Ramblas was a seasonal riverbed that marked the western edge of medieval Barcelona with the city walls on one side and a market on the other. By the time the 16th-century convent of Sant Josep was torn down in 1836 to make room for a new iron structure, the city had grown up, and Las Ramblas was not merely the main city drainage but its mile-long artery.

When I arrive at La Boqueria, I make a slow, meandering loop through the stalls to see what looks freshest and best. About the size of a football field and resembling an old train station, it offers, simply, nearly everything edible anyone could desire. Around a circular core of fish and seafood—broad-faced monkfish, ink-stained squid laid out on ice, whiting with their tails clamped into their long serrated jaws, buckets of dark slippery eels from the rice fields of the Ebro Delta—are the rest of the hundreds of other stalls. Long counters of

Manchego cheeses. Tubs of olives, dipped with round slotted spoons, ladled into plastic sacks. Hanging cured hams, sliced thin with long, slender knives sharp as scalpels. Chickens, partridges, quail, ducks, and pheasants dangling by their feet in full feathered dress. Fruits that define the seasons: blood oranges in late winter, sweet green plums that last only a few weeks between spring and summer, fig-size pears at the end of June. In autumn, *bolets* (wild mushrooms) so plentiful and various at Llorenç Petràs's stall that only a mycophile could possibly identify them all.

Once I have done a complete loop, I settle on one of the dozen or so stools at Pinotxo. Albert gives me a tired, hang-dog greeting as he adds something to a sizzling pan or gives a stiff shake to one of the large pots on the stove. I've learned a lot from Albert over the years, watching his slacker's ease and confident precision at the stove. There are no shortcuts in this kitchen, no mise en place with dozens of prepared ingredients that simply need to be assembled. Dishes have foundations (usually a sofrito) and are structured upward. If he or Jordi need an ingredient as they cook, they only have to shout to one of the nearby stalls.

As I linger over breakfast, watching them cook and listening to the banter between them and those on the stools beside me (inevitably about the local *futbol* team, Barça), I begin to plan a meal or two in my head, inspired by what looks good in the market.

Once I have wiped my plate clean with bread—something that horrifies my wife, but here I nearly always come alone, so I do it with pleasure, for the best flavors are concentrated in those traces of oil—I order un tallat and on the paper placemat begin penciling down the ingredients I need. When my coffee is finished, I tear away the corner of the placemat and head back through the stalls, this time to buy.

# Gandia-Style Fideuà / Fideuà de Gandia (Valencia, Spain)

Fideuà can be loosely described as a noodle version of paella; the pasta is not boiled separately but absorbs the flavors of the pan. The most famous fideuà comes from Gandia (south of Valencia), where it was said to have been invented over a century ago by a local fisherman. One day, in the middle of the Mediterranean, the cook went to prepare the midday seafood paella only to discover that he had forgotten the rice, and so he used fideos instead. Every June, Gandia hosts an annual fideuà contest. Contestants must use the official, albeit minimalist, recipe (the ingredient list is more important than directions). I have only deviated in the stock—officially, it's made with *moralla* (a small stock fish of the wrasse family), but use whatever good, fresh white fish the sea offers up—and added some flavor-boosting cuttlefish. The allioli isn't on the recipe either, but it goes too perfectly with fideuà not to dollop on top.

| | |
|---|---|
| 7 | tablespoons extra-virgin olive oil |
| 1 | leek (white and tender green parts only), chopped |
| 1 | carrot, roughly chopped |
| 1 | stalk celery, roughly chopped |
| 2 | pounds assorted soup fish or the heads (gills removed) and bones of monkfish or another flavorful firm, white-fleshed fish |
| 9 | cups water |
| 1 | small bunch parsley |
| 2 | garlic cloves, minced |
| 2 | medium onions, finely chopped |
| 2 | tomatoes, peeled, seeded, and finely chopped |

| | |
|---|---|
| | Salt |
| 4 | uncooked Dublin Bay prawns or scampi with shells |
| 8 | large or jumbo uncooked head-on shrimp with shells |
| 8 | ounces cuttlefish or squid, cleaned and cut into bite-sized pieces |
| 4 | ounces deboned monkfish, cut into thick cubes |
| 1 | teaspoon sweet pimentón (paprika) |
| 20 | saffron threads, dry roasted and ground |
| 14 | ounces medium-thick (Number 2) fideos |
| | Allioli (page 57) |

Prepare a fish stock. In a stockpot or another large pot over medium heat, heat 1 tablespoon of the oil. Add the leek, carrot, and celery, and cook until they begin to release their juices, about 5 minutes. Add the fish and cover with the water. Bring to a simmer, reduce the heat to medium-low and simmer for 30 minutes. Remove from the heat, add the parsley, and let it infuse as the stock cools. Strain through a sieve and discard the solids.

Meanwhile, prepare a sofrito. In a heavy cazuela or sauté pan or skillet over medium-low heat, heat 2 tablespoons of the oil. Add the garlic and onions, and cook until the onions are soft, 5 to 10 minutes. Add the tomatoes, 2 tablespoons of the simmering fish stock, and

CONTINUED

2 pinches of salt, and cook until the sofrito darkens and thickens, 10 to 15 minutes.

Pour the stock over the sofrito and simmer over low heat for 20 minutes to reduce. Pass through a food mill or blender to purée. There should be at least 6 cups.

In a clean saucepan over high heat, bring the puréed stock to a boil, reduce heat to low, cover, and keep hot.

In a 16- to 18-inch paella pan over medium heat, heat the remaining 4 tablespoons of oil. Add the prawns and shrimp and cook, stirring continuously, until browned. Transfer to a platter. In the same oil, add the cuttlefish and cook, stirring frequently, until it has browned and released its liquid, about 5 minutes. Add the monkfish and cook until browned. Keep stirring to make sure nothing in the pan burns.

Add the pimentón, saffron, and fideos. Stir thoroughly to coat completely. Pour in 6 cups of the stock and bring to a boil, stirring to scrape anything that has stuck to the bottom of the pan. Taste for seasoning and adjust as needed. Cook, uncovered, for 4 minutes. Distribute the prawns and shrimp across the pasta, and then continue to cook until the pasta is tender and the liquid has been absorbed.

Serve with the allioli.

# Grandma's Penne Pasta with Tomato, Fresh Sausage, and Chorizo / Macarrons de l'Iaia (Catalonia, Spain)

Whenever all nine grandchildren assemble at my mother-in-law's home for lunch, *Iaia* ("grandma" in Catalan) is sure to make *macarrons*—penne pasta with tomato sauce and nuggets of fresh sausage links. It's the cliché dish that all Catalan kids (and adults!) love. This dish is a staple not only at grandma's house but also in country restaurants and even weddings. It's a surefire hit.

| | | | | |
|---|---|---|---|---|
| 3 | tablespoons extra-virgin olive oil | | 4 | tomatoes, peeled, seeded, and finely chopped |
| 1 | medium onion, finely chopped | | 2 | ounces Spanish chorizo, cut into small pieces |
| 8 | ounces unsweetened fresh pork sausages links, pulled from the casing and pinched into marble-size pieces | | 1 ¼ | pounds penne pasta |
| | Salt | | 2 | ounces grated Emmental or "Swiss" cheese |

Prepare a sofrito. In a large cazuela, heavy-based sauté pan, or skillet over medium-low heat, heat the oil. Add the onion, sausage, and a pinch of salt and cook, stirring frequently, until the sausage gets some color and the onion is soft and translucent, about 10 minutes. Add the tomatoes and chorizo and continue to cook, stirring occasionally, until the tomatoes have darkened and lost their acidity, about 15 minutes. Add a few tablespoons of water if the mixture looks about to dry out.

Meanwhile, in a pasta pot, bring 4 quarts of water to a boil and add 4 teaspoons of salt. When the water returns to a rolling boil, add the pasta. Cook, stirring from time to time to keep the pasta from clumping together, until al dente. Drain but do not rinse, shaking off any water that clings to the pasta.

Return the pasta to the pot. Add the sofrito and cheese and blend until the pasta is thoroughly coated and the cheese has melted. Serve in warm bowls.

# Cannelloni Stuffed with Spinach, Pine Nuts, and Raisins / Canelons d'espinacs (Catalonia, Spain)

Each Christmas my mother-in-law prepares upward of one hundred cannelloni stuffed with ground meat as the centerpiece of the family lunch. She covers them with a thin béchamel sauce, tops them with cheese, and then slides the whole dish into the oven for a nice gratin. They take hours to prepare, and we devour them within minutes.

In our house, we eat cannelloni year-round, but always stuffed with spinach, pine nuts, and raisins. A hard-boiled egg bulks up the filling, though the egg should be smashed enough to go largely unnoticed. They may not take quite as long to make, but they are devoured just as fast.

|   |   |
|---|---|
|   | Salt |
| 20 | cannelloni sheets (see page 97) or lasagna square broken into 2 ¾- to 3-inch-square pieces |
| ¼ | cup small seedless raisins |
| 1 | hard-boiled egg, peeled |
| 1 ½ | tablespoons extra-virgin olive oil |
| 1 | medium onion, finely chopped |
| 3 | tablespoons pine nuts |

|   |   |
|---|---|
| 1 | pound fresh spinach leaves, washed and shredded |
|   | Freshly ground pepper |
| 3 ½ | tablespoons butter |
| 2 | tablespoons flour |
| 3 | cups milk |
| 1 | pinch nutmeg |
| 2 | ounces grated Emmental or "Swiss" cheese |

In a pasta pot, bring 4 quarts of water to a boil and add 4 teaspoons of salt. When the water returns to a rolling boil, add the cannelloni squares one by one. Boil, stirring carefully to keep the squares from sticking together yet without tearing them, until al dente, usually 12 to 16 minutes but follow the directions on the package. Transfer with a slotted spoon to a bowl of cold water. Once cooled, drain the pasta and spread out, in a single layer, on a large marble surface or a table covered with clean kitchen towels.

Meanwhile, soak the raisins in tepid water for 15 minutes; drain. In a large bowl, mash the egg with the back of a fork.

In a small sauté pan or skillet over medium-low heat, heat the oil. Add the onion and cook until it begins to soften, about 5 minutes. Add the pine nuts and raisins and cook until the onion is soft, the pine nuts golden, and the raisins plump, about 5 minutes. Transfer to the bowl with the egg.

In a large pot, bring 3 quarts of water to a boil and add 1 teaspoon of salt. Add the spinach leaves and boil until tender, about 6 minutes. Drain in a colander. When cool enough to handle, press out the excess moisture from the spinach. Transfer the spinach to the egg mixture, season with salt and pepper, and mix thoroughly.

Begin rolling the cannelloni. Place a heaped spoonful of the spinach mix on each square and roll into tubes. Place side by side, seam-side up in a shallow rectangular ovenproof baking dish. (Placing the seams facing up will allow the cooked cannelloni to be removed and served without coming apart.)

Prepare a thin béchamel sauce. In a heavy saucepan over medium heat, melt the butter. Add the flour and cook until the flour loses its raw taste, about 3 minutes. Add the milk slowly. Starting at medium heat and gradually reducing to low, cook, whisking frequently, until thickened, around 30 minutes. Stir in the nutmeg at the very end.

Preheat the oven broiler.

Pour the béchamel sauce evenly over the cannelloni. Top with the grated cheese. Place in the oven and broil until the cheese is brown and slightly crispy.

To serve, carefully remove the cannelloni from the baking dish without breaking. Divide evenly among plates and spoon over top any remaining béchamel sauce.

## Orzo with Brown Butter and Cheese / Manestra me voutiro kai tiri (Greece)

Orzo is a much-loved pasta in Greece, where it is called *manestra* or *kritharaki*. As one friend said when we were talking about our childhoods: "I remember a lot of orzo." This is the Greek version of that simple standby "pasta with cheese and butter." Other types of pasta work, but orzo is a favorite.

|    | Salt |
|----|------|
| 14 | ounces orzo |
| ¼  | cup butter |

|   |   |
|---|---|
| 1 | garlic clove, minced |
| 2 | ounces freshly grated aged kasseri or mizithra cheese |
|   | Freshly ground pepper |

In a pasta pot, bring 4 quarts of water to a boil and add 4 teaspoons of salt. When the water returns to a rolling boil, add the pasta. Cook, stirring from time to time to keep the pasta from clumping together, until al dente. Drain but do not rinse, shaking off any water that clings to the pasta. Return the pasta to the pot.

Meanwhile, in a small saucepan over low heat, melt the butter and cook until caramel colored, about 10 minutes. Watch carefully that it does not burn. Remove from the heat and either skim off the solids or strain off the clear liquid; discard the solids. Add the garlic, stir, and let infuse in the hot butter for 1 to 2 minutes.

Pour the butter over the pasta and toss with the cheese. Serve in warm bowls, seasoned with salt and pepper to taste.

# Baked Lamb and Orzo Casserole / Arni yiouvetsi (Greece)

The "yiouvetsi" in the recipe's name refers to the terra-cotta casserole in which this classic lamb dish is traditionally roasted. The orzo is sprinkled into the pan toward the end to suck up and swell with the flavors of the lamb. Individual cuts of lamb shoulder can be used, but a tender, small whole leg of baby lamb is preferable. Have the butcher cut all the way through the bone, leaving the bottom strip of meat intact to keep the shape of the leg to allow for easier serving.

| | |
|---|---|
| ¼ | cup extra-virgin olive oil |
| | Juice of 1 lemon |
| 1 | heaping teaspoon oregano |
| | Salt and freshly ground pepper |
| 1 | bone-in leg of baby lamb (3 to 4 pounds), cut through the bone in 6 places but still attached |
| 2 | garlic cloves, minced |

| | |
|---|---|
| 1 | medium onion, finely chopped |
| 3 | ripe medium tomatoes, cored, seeded, and puréed |
| ½ | cup water |
| 3 | cups Chicken Stock (page 33) |
| 1 | cup orzo |
| 1 | ounce freshly grated kefalotiri cheese |

Preheat the oven to 350°F and set the oven rack in the lower third of the oven.

In a bowl, whisk together the oil, lemon juice, and oregano; season with salt and pepper.

Place the lamb in a large terra-cotta yiouvetsi, ovenproof Dutch oven, or roasting pan. Brush about three-fourths of the liquid over the lamb. Sprinkle the garlic, onion, and tomatoes around its base and then dribble the water over the vegetables.

Place in the oven and roast for 15 minutes. Baste the lamb with the remaining oil-lemon mixture. Continue to roast for another 40 minutes, basting every 15 minutes or so, and turn the lamb over at the halfway mark of the 40 minutes. Add more water if the tomato sauce looks about to dry out.

Meanwhile, bring the stock to a boil in a saucepan.

Turn the lamb again at the end of the 40 minutes. Pour the boiling stock around the base of the lamb and scrape away any browned bits from the bottom of the pan. Sprinkle the orzo into the liquid and stir. Cook for 30 minutes or until the lamb is done and the pasta is tender. Add more water, if needed, as the pasta cooks.

Turn the oven to "broil."

Sprinkle the grated cheese over the pasta and return the pan to the oven until the cheese is melted, about 5 minutes.

Cut the meat into thick slices and serve alongside the orzo.

## Tlitli with Meatballs / Tlitli aux boulettes de viande (Algeria)

Algerian *tlitli*, a short, slender ovoid pasta similar to orzo, are cooked in different ways. One method treats them like couscous and steams them in a couscoussier before tossing with sauce, while another, which I prefer for this recipe, browns them in the pan and then adds the sauce, which is absorbed by the pasta in the style of Greek Baked Lamb and Orzo Casserole (page 145) and Gandia-style Fideuà (page 139). The final texture is moist and velvety, the flavors delicately hinting of cinnamon. Without a doubt, it's our favorite North African pasta dish.

| | |
|---|---|
| 1 | pound piece bone-in veal such as shank (osso buco) or lamb |
| 1 | plus ½ medium onions, grated and divided as such |
| 3 | tablespoons extra-virgin olive oil |
| ¼ | teaspoon sweet paprika (piment doux) |
| | Cayenne pepper (piment fort) |
| | Cinnamon |
| | Salt and freshly ground pepper |
| 5 | cups water |

| | |
|---|---|
| 8 | ounces ground veal or lamb |
| 1 | large egg |
| 2 | tablespoons finely chopped fresh flat-leaf parsley |
| ½ | Scant cup breadcrumbs |
| 1 | cup canned chickpeas, drained and rinsed |
| 12 | ounces tlitli, langues d'oiseaux, or orzo |
| 2 | hard-boiled eggs, peeled and quartered lengthwise |

Put the veal shank and 1 of the onions in the bottom of a large pot. Add 1 tablespoon of the oil and swirl to coat. Cook over medium heat until the meat is browned and the onion begins to soften, about 5 minutes. Season with the sweet paprika, a pinch of cayenne pepper, a pinch each of cinnamon, salt, and pepper. Add the water and bring to a boil. Reduce the heat to low, cover, and cook for 30 minutes.

Meanwhile, prepare and fry the meatballs. In a large bowl, combine the ground veal, the remaining ½ onion, the egg, and parsley; season with salt, pepper, and a pinch of cinnamon. Add the breadcrumbs and knead the mixture into a consistent paste that will hold its shape. Form into golf ball–size meatballs.

In a large sauté pan or skillet over medium heat, heat the remaining 2 tablespoons of oil and brown the meatballs, turning over gently. Transfer with a slotted spoon to a paper towel–lined plate to drain. Remove the pan from the heat but do not discard the oil.

Add the meatballs and the chickpeas to the broth. Shake the pot to settle them into the liquid. Cover and cook for 20 minutes.

Remove the meatballs and chickpeas with a slotted spoon and transfer to a bowl; cover and keep warm.

CONTINUED

In the sauté pan over medium heat and using the reserved oil, add the tlitli and cook until it begins to brown, about 5 minutes. Pour in 4 cups of broth and cook until the pasta is tender and the broth has been absorbed, 15 to 18 minutes. Add more broth (or hot water) if needed.

To serve, spread the tlitli out on a platter. Top with the meatballs, chickpeas, and veal shank. Garnish with the hard-boiled eggs.

# Meat-Filled Manti with Garlic Yogurt Sauce / Mantı (Turkey)

What a perfect combination of flavors! Tiny fresh pasta packets, holding just a pinch of thyme-flavored meat, topped with garlicky yogurt, a drizzle of chile-infused melted butter, and a fine dusting of dried mint and sumac. Originating most likely in China, *mantı* traveled across the Central Asian steppes and the Anatolia region toward Istanbul, where it was a central dish in 15th-century Ottoman cuisine. It remains a Turkish favorite. I've enjoyed them in Istanbul eateries but the best I've tasted came from a corner grocery store in Balat, one of the city's conservative neighborhoods that run up the westside of the Golden Horn. Spying both fresh and dried *mantı*, I asked the woman behind the counter if they were the same, meaning the filling. "No," she said. "The fresh, I made. The dried, machine made." Needless to say, I bought the fresh.

FOR THE PASTA DOUGH:

| | |
|---|---|
| 2 | cups tipo "00" flour or American unbleached all-purpose flour, plus more for dusting |
| 1 | egg |
| ⅓ | cup warm water |
| ¼ | teaspoon salt |

FOR THE FILLING:

| | |
|---|---|
| 8 | ounces ground veal or lamb |
| ½ | teaspoon dried thyme |
| 2 | cups natural yogurt |
| 2 | garlic cloves, minced |
| ¼ | cup butter |

Salt and freshly ground pepper

Chili flakes

Sumac

Dried mint

Prepare the dough: Use the quantities listed here and follow the directions on page 101 with these additions—after whisking the egg, gradually work the water and salt into the dough. Cover and rest the dough for 30 minutes, reknead for 10 minutes, and then cover and rest for a final 15 minutes.

While the pasta rests, prepare the filling: In a large bowl, combine the veal and thyme and season with salt and pepper. Knead into a consistent paste.

In another bowl, whisk the yogurt together with the garlic. Cover and refrigerate until ready to use.

Divide the pasta into 4 equal pieces; cover with plastic wrap until ready to use. Divide the filling into 4 equal parts.

Roll out one piece of the pasta on the thinnest setting in a pasta machine or by hand following the directions on page 101. (Ideally use a traditional Turkish *oklava*—a long, smooth wooden stick about 3/4 inch in diameter—to roll the dough into almost paper-thin sheets.)

Lay the sheet on a clean bed sheet or kitchen towels. With a pasta cutter, cut the pasta lengthwise into $1^{1}/_{4}$- to $1^{1}/_{2}$-inch-wide strips and then cut crosswise to make squares. Spoon $^{1}/_{8}$ teaspoon of filling in the middle of each square.

Taking one square between the fingers, fold it into a small parcel by pinching together the corners, letting the top of the dough form a cross between the tips of the fingers. The shape should look like squat, old-fashioned money bags.

Place them back on the sheet. Repeat with the rest of the squares and filling, laying them out on the sheet without touching each other.

Roll out another piece of dough and repeat until all of the dough and filling are used up. Cover the mantı with plastic and refrigerate if not used within an hour.

In a large pasta pot, bring 4 quarts of water to a rolling boil and add 4 teaspoons of salt. Add half of the mantı and simmer until al dente and the filling is cooked, about 5 minutes. Scoop out with a slotted spoon and transfer to a serving dish. Cover and keep warm while cooking the remaining mantı.

Meanwhile, in a small saucepan over medium heat, melt the butter. Add a generous pinch of chili flakes and remove from the heat.

Divide the mantı among warm bowls. Cover with the yogurt and drizzle some butter over each. Serve with the remaining yogurt on the side as well as small dishes of sumac, dried mint, and chili flakes to dust over as desired.

# **Kushary** (Cairo, Egypt)

Egyptian *kushary* is made with pasta, rice, lentils, chickpeas, a tangy tomato sauce, and sweet fried onions, an almost improbable combination that's surprisingly good. It's also cheap and filling, which were more important during my first trips to Cairo back in the early and mid-1990s, when I ate it daily from colorful street carts for pennies a bowl. These days, even if taste trumps absolute cheapness in priorities, kushary remains a favorite, and I happily splurge and pay five Egyptian pounds (about one U.S. dollar) for a bowl of the city's best at Abou Tarek, an enormous, over-lit emporium dedicated to this uniquely Egyptian dish.

Though no part is complicated, kushary takes time to prepare because there are so many separate elements. But assembling it is easy and, if done at the table, festive.

|   |   |   |   |
|---|---|---|---|
|   | Salt | 1 | cup tubetti, ditali, or another short, round tube pasta |
| 1 | cup dried brown lentils, washed | 1 | tablespoon butter |
| 3 | tablespoons olive oil | 2 | cups short- or medium-grain rice |
| 4 | medium onions, 1 very finely chopped and the others cut into very thin slices | 3 | ounces vermicelli or angel-hair pasta, crushed or broken into ½- to 1-inch-long pieces, or thin fideos (about 1 scant cup) |
| 4 | garlic cloves, minced |   |   |
| 6 | tomatoes, halved, seeded, and grated (about 2 cups of pulp; see page 162) | 6 | tablespoons oil for frying |
| 1 | teaspoon white wine vinegar | 1 | cup canned chickpeas, drained and rinsed |
|   |   |   | Hot chili sauce |
| 3 | ounces spaghetti, broken in half | 3 | lemons, quartered |

In a large pot, bring 5 cups of water to a boil. Add 1 teaspoon of salt and the lentils, return to a boil and then cover and cook over medium heat until tender, about 30 minutes. Keep warm.

In a sauté pan or skillet over medium-low heat, heat 2 tablespoons of the olive oil. Add the chopped onion and cook until the onion begins to soften, about 5 minutes. Add the garlic and cook until it begins to color, another few minutes. Add the tomatoes and cook until they have darkened, 20 to 30 minutes, depending on their ripeness.

Add the vinegar and cook for another 3 to 5 minutes. Purée the sauce in a blender or pass it through a food mill, and then return it to the pan. Stir in just enough warm water to make the sauce loose and runny. Cover and keep warm until serving.

Meanwhile, in a pasta pot, bring 4 quarts of water to a boil and add 4 teaspoons of salt. When the water returns to a rolling boil, add the broken spaghetti and tubetti. Cook, stirring from time to time to keep the pasta from clumping together, until al dente. Drain but do not rinse, shaking off any water that clings to the pasta. Transfer to a bowl and set aside.

Bring an abundant amount of water to a boil in a large pot. Add a pinch of salt, the butter, and the rice, and boil until al dente, about 16 minutes. Drain, briefly rinse under running water, and drain again. Transfer to a large bowl. Meanwhile, heat the remaining 1 tablespoon of olive oil in a small skillet. Add the vermicelli and cook over medium heat until browned, about 2 minutes. Add ³/₄ cup of water and cook, uncovered, until the vermicelli is soft and the water is absorbed, 3 or 4 minutes. Add more water if needed. Transfer to the bowl with the rice. Mix together and fluff with a fork.

In a sauté pan or skillet over medium heat, heat the frying oil. Add the sliced onions and cook over low heat until they become soft and translucent, about 15 minutes. Increase the heat to high and cook until the onions are caramel brown, 7 to 10 minutes. Watch carefully that they do not burn, especially in the last few minutes. Remove with a slotted spoon and spread out on a paper towel–lined plate to drain.

In a small saucepan over medium heat, warm the chickpeas.

Assemble the kushary individually. In each bowl, add a ladleful of pasta and then form a mound. Add a ladleful of rice to it and remound. Top with some lentils and ladle over tomato sauce. Place a spoonful of chickpeas and some fried onions on top of that. Serve with the remaining tomato sauce in a bowl on the side with the chili sauce and lemons to squeeze over the top.

SERVES 4

# Sweet Vermicelli / Chariya seffa (Morocco)

Sweet rice dishes are common all over the Mediterranean, but sweet pasta ones less so. Here's one, though, that isn't for dessert; rather, it's a northern Morocco dinner dish. (It also makes an excellent snack.) The noodles are steamed in a couscoussier and then tossed with sugar and cinnamon. Dunking the *chariya* into boiling water between steamings rinses off some of the starches so the noodles don't clump together. Although retaining a superior firm consistency in the couscoussier, the noodles can be simply boiled until al dente.

| | | | | |
|---|---|---|---|---|
| 8 | cups water | | 1 | tablespoon butter or smen |
| | Salt | | 3 | tablespoons sugar |
| 8 | ounces vermicelli or angel-hair pasta, crushed or broken into ½- to 1-inch-long pieces, or thin fideos | | | Cinnamon for dusting |
| 2 | tablespoons of extra-virgin olive oil | | | |

In the bottom of a couscoussier, bring the water to a boil. Add a generous pinch of salt

Toss the vermicelli with 1 tablespoon of the oil, coating well. Transfer to the steaming basket. Once the water is boiling, place the basket firmly over the couscoussier. Steam for 15 minutes, beginning the timing when the steams rises up through the surface of the pasta.

Tip the vermicelli into the boiling water below, using a spatula to get any pasta that sticks to the sides. Immediately drain the pasta, reserving the hot water. Pour the hot water back into the bottom of the couscoussier and return it to a boil.

Drizzle the remaining 1 tablespoon of oil over the vermicelli, mixing until the pasta is thoroughly coated. Place the basket back on top of the couscoussier and steam the pasta for a second time for 15 minutes, beginning the count once the steam rises through the surface.

Tip the vermicelli into a wide serving bowl. Mix in the butter and sugar, separating any pasta that's clumped together.

Divide evenly among bowls, dust with cinnamon, and serve warm.

# Vermicelli with Milk and Cinnamon /
# Vermicelle au lait à la canelle (Morocco)

This is another sweet pasta dish from northern Morocco that's served at dinnertime. Some like it with plenty of milk; others like slightly less. Serve warm in bowls with spoons.

| | | |
|---|---|---|
| 4 | cups whole milk | Orange blossom water (optional) |
| 3 | tablespoons sugar | Cinnamon for dusting |
| | Salt | |
| 3 | ounces vermicelli or angel-hair pasta, crushed or broken into ½- to 1-inch-long pieces, or thin fideos (about 1 scant cup) | |

In a saucepan over medium heat, bring the milk to a simmer, stirring so that it does not stick to the bottom. Add the sugar, a pinch of salt, and the vermicelli. Lower the heat to medium-low and cook, stirring frequently, until the vermicelli is soft, 2 to 4 minutes. Stir in a dash of orange blossom water (if using).

Divide evenly among bowls, dust with cinnamon, and serve warm.

# COUSCOUS

# Mediterranean Couscous Primer

## Brief History and Overview

*Couscous* means both the tiny, hard pellets rolled from (usually) durum wheat semolina as well as the whole dish. Couscous as a "grain" is the Maghreb's long-standing staple; couscous as a dish is the region's most celebrated and delectable culinary legacy.

Although generally attributed to indigenous Berbers, who began making couscous with barley and acorn flour, it was the Arabs who transformed it into a distinct regional cuisine across North Africa after they introduced hard durum wheat into the Maghreb. Food historians and linguists place the development of durum wheat couscous between the 11th and 13th centuries. (The word *couscous* comes from the Arabic *kuskus*, which is derived from the Berber *seksu*.)

The beadlike grains are steamed two or three times in the perforated top of a two-tiered pot, known as a *couscoussier*, by the aromatic vapors of the stew cooking in the bottom section. Before, between, and after the steamings, the grains are spritzed with water, rubbed between the palms, and worked with oil, *smen* (clarified and preserved butter), or butter to keep them from clumping. The result is light and fluffy grains that are individual and tender but not mushy.

## Regional Differences

If couscous offers a unifying regional identity, it also acts as a takeoff point for national distinction. The differences lie in the flavors of the stew or broth.

In Morocco, stews tend to have subtle but complex spice flavorings—blending, say, saffron with turmeric, coriander, ginger, and nutmeg—and often combine the sweet and savory—quince and lamb, dates and squab, caramelized onions and chicken. Moroccan cuisine draws on a diverse bounty of local products and on elements from its multilayered history, incorporating a band of disparate influences—from the Moors and the Jews who fled Spain in the 15th and 16th centuries to the refined, sophisticated cooking of the royal palace.

Algerian couscous tends to be humbler, marked by robust, rustic heartiness. The broth is almost always based on tomatoes and colored red with tomato paste, and it includes plenty of vegetables and legumes (chickpeas are ubiquitous) but often just a handful of spices—sweet paprika and hot chili pepper, sometimes cinnamon, or ground coriander seeds when the dish includes fresh fava beans. Lamb or chicken help flavor most broths; though, along the coastline, cooks prepare fish couscouses in red broths as well as tomato-less "white" ones.

While fish couscouses are also prepared along Tunisia's lengthy coastline—sea bream with quince is a winter favorite—lamb dominates stews, whether helping flavor a vegetable one or playing the protagonist, crowning a mound of grains, and topped with dried fruits and nuts. Tunisian couscous stews stand out for their redness (tomato concentrate!), high spicing, and liberal addition of harissa chile paste (see page 162).

Between couscous's versatility and its strong role in cultural traditions, North Africans immigrants have carried it all over the globe. In France, with colonial ties to the region and decades of immigration, couscous has taken hold and is now one of the country's most popular foods—for those with Maghrebi roots as well as those without. A big push toward couscous integration came after Algeria gained independence from France in 1962. At that time, one million *pieds-noirs* (literally "black feet"; Algerian-born French settlers, some with families who had settled as far back as 1830) and Sephardic Jews were expelled from the newly independent country and settled largely along the French Mediterranean.

Couscous also exists in the European Mediterranean as a long-established local dish in Sicily. It endures along the western shore, most likely as a remnant of the island's two hundred years of Moorish rule (878 to 1091). Traditional Sicilian *cuscus* is prepared with fish and flavored, most notably, with bay leaf and cinnamon. The grains are steamed separately, soaked in the broth for an hour, and then served moist but unadorned. On the tiny nearby island of Pantelleria, a sauté of eggplant, peppers, and zucchini, as well as flakes of fish, top fish broth–soaked couscous grains.

## Types and Sizes

Couscous comes in a variety of types and sizes. Here are some details on the main ones.

**FRESHLY ROLLED:** Couscous is made from scratch by rubbing and rolling two different calibers of ground semolina with a touch of salted water in a large, sloped-edge bowl known as a *gsaa* or *sahfah* (or *mafaradda* in Sicily) into tiny pellets. The "grains" are sifted through a round sieve called a *ghorbal* and into a woven basket to dry; larger pellets get rerolled until they're small enough to pass through the sieve or are used as *berkoukès* (see facing page). Making couscous from scratch is a difficult, time-consuming process less frequently done these days, especially with excellent commercial brands of prerolled (which isn't to say precooked) couscous filling local market shelves. I've met a number of people in North Africa who once rolled couscous frequently but now do so just occasionally and always in a festive, family atmosphere.

The only company producing hand-rolled grains on a commercial level that I am aware of is La Maison Lahlou in the mountainous Kabylie region east of Algiers (see page 181). Maison Lahlou sells these domestically and, for the moment at least, exports only to France.

**STANDARD:** Standard couscous is ready-rolled but not precooked. It needs to be washed or moistened with water and allowed to sit and swell before being steamed two or three times for a total of 45 to 60 minutes. Between steamings, it's rested and any clumps worked out. Most North African and French brands are sold either in bulk or in 1-kilogram plastic sacks (precooked "instant" couscous tends to come in 500-gram and 1-kilogram boxes). To find standard couscous, look in Middle Eastern groceries, health food stores, or in the Sources on page 211.

**PRECOOKED "INSTANT":** These days, the most commonly found (and used) couscous in North America (and Europe) is precooked "instant" couscous, which is ready, the packages claim, "in 5 minutes." Every North African cook whom I know, as well as purists around the world, shun it, claiming it does not have the fluffiness or delicate texture of the standard double- or triple-steamed grains. But, if handled properly (see page 167), "instant" couscous can be quite light and fluffy. At home, I prepare both types, depending on my time and mood and what's in the pantry.

**NON-WHEAT VARIETIES:** The majority of couscous made and eaten today is from hard durum wheat. There are also variations made from barley, millet, acorn, corn, and rice. Of these, barley is the most widespread and remains popular in Berber-dominated regions. Known as *sakssou al belboula* in Berber and *couscous d'ogre* in French, barley couscous is darker and nuttier than its semolina cousin and combines especially well with more rustic-flavored couscouses. Along with La Maison Lahlou in Algeria, the Moroccan company Dari produces it; Sahadi's market in Brooklyn carries the Dari brand (see Sources page 211). Two excellent restaurants to try barley couscous are Dar Lahlou in Algiers and La Fémina in the center of Marseille.

**FINE AND MEDIUM GRAIN:** Medium grain is the most common size of couscous, followed by fine grain. Certain dishes call for a specific size—sweet couscouses often use fine—but the choice remains mostly a matter of preference. Being larger, medium grain has more bite to it.

**BERKOUKÈS, MHAMSA, AND MHAMMAS:** Large-sized couscous is known as *berkoukès* in Algeria, *mhamsa* in Morocco, and *mhammas* in Tunisia; in French, they're sometimes called *petits plombs*. It is produced both like large-sized couscous as well as tiny pellets of pasta, and can be steamed like couscous or boiled like pasta. The most common size is a bit smaller than a peppercorn, though they come as small as buckshot and almost as big as a pencil eraser.

**FREGOLA:** These large, peppercorn-size beads of couscous from Sardinia are made by rolling durum semolina with salted water in a circular motion. The pellets are dried and toasted in the oven, where they obtain their distinctive brownish color, nutty taste, and slightly textured surface. In coastal southern Sardinia around Cagliari, fregola pellets are typically simmered in clam broth, while inland they are served with a sauce of tomatoes and fresh sausage. They're also called *fregula*.

**MOGHRABBIYEH:** The name of this large-size Lebanese couscous clearly acknowledges its Maghrebi origins. Once steamed for hours, these pellets are now simmered in a chicken- or lamb-based broth. Moghrabbiyeh is also eaten in neighboring Syria, though much less frequently.

## Techniques and Secrets
### COUSCOUSSIER
This two-level pot—usually called by its French name, *couscoussier* (*kiskis* in Arabic)—is used to cook both the stew and the couscous grains. The stew goes in the pot-bellied bottom section, and the grains are placed in the perforated top section that fits tightly over it. As the stew simmers, the steam is forced up through the holes and cooks the grains while bestowing them with the flavors of the broth.

Though traditionally terra-cotta, couscoussiers these days are most often metal, sometimes sturdy stainless steel, or even copper, though usually lighter, cheaper metals. My own inexpensive couscoussier, bought half a dozen years ago in a Moroccan *halal* butcher shop in Barcelona, remains in excellent condition after countless uses.

In Jerba, a small island just off the southern Tunisian coast, couscoussiers have a third tier between the stew and the grains. It's especially ideal for fish, which can cook without flaking apart in the broth.

### SUBSTITUTING A COUSCOUSSIER
A large pot with a colander or steamer basket fitted over the top works well as a substitution for a couscoussier. There needs to be plenty of space for the water or stew below and a tight seal between the pot and the basket to keep the steam from escaping.

## AMOUNTS

One pound of uncooked couscous (about 2¹/₂ cups) serves about three people in North Africa, though roughly double that elsewhere. Feel free to prepare more couscous than called for in these recipes. A massive heaped mound is always impressive, and leftover couscous is easily turned into a salad, a side dish, or sweetened for a snack.

## SEALING A COUSCOUSSIER

The two sections of a couscoussier—the bottom pot where the stew cooks and the perforated top basket where the couscous steams—need to have a good seal between them so that all of the steam is forced up through the grains. Traditional recipes call for a band of flour and water to be painted around the joint. But this is messy and impractical. A simpler and cleaner method is to place a thin strip of aluminum foil where the pot and the basket join. (In Morocco, many cooks do this with a supermarket plastic sack instead of foil.) Alternatively, take a long length of aluminum foil, fold it into a belt, wrap it around the joint, twist the two ends of foil together, and gradually cinch it snug, working the foil tightly around the edges. To remove the basket between steamings, simply uncinch the foil belt; once the basket is replaced, recinch it.

## BROTH

At the end of cooking, there should be about ³/₄ to 1 cup of broth per person in order to moisten the grains as well as ladle over the couscous when eating. Stir in some water at the end if desired, though be careful not to dilute the flavors.

## TOMATOES AND TOMATO CONCENTRATE

Tomatoes are fundamental to Tunisian and Algerian couscous broths. Tomato concentrate is commonly used for coloring. Look for double concentrate; I especially like Italian *doppio concentrato di pomodoro* sold in metal tubes.

Fresh tomatoes should be peeled and finely chopped or grated. Reserve all of the juice when seeding—I place a small strainer over a glass—and add it, along with the tomatoes, to the dish.

To peel and chop: Fill a large basin with iced water. Cut the core from the tomatoes and make an "X" mark on the bottom with the tip of a knife. In a large pot, bring an abundant amount of water to a rolling boil, add the tomatoes, and boil until the skins begin to split. Remove the tomatoes and plunge them into the cold water to stop any further cooking. Once they have cooled, remove with a slotted spoon, drain, and peel. Finely chop.

To grate: Cut the tomatoes in half crosswise and run a finger through the seed cavity, scraping most of the seeds. Cupping the tomato in one hand, slowly grate on a box grater until skin peels back and all the flesh is grated away. Discard the flattened skin.

## SMEN

Clarified and preserved butter worked into couscous adds flavor but also keeps the grains separate. It's similar to ghee, though more pungent; the smell ranges from cheesy to rancid. Clarified (but not necessarily preserved) butter is also used in Egyptian, Syrian, and Lebanese kitchens. Substitute ghee or butter.

## HARISSA

Harissa is Tunisia's omnipresent condiment. Made from dried local chile peppers, garlic, olive oil, coriander, caraway, and salt, it's ground into a thick paste.

Various types of these chile peppers, brought from the Americas in the 16th century by the Spanish and perfectly adapted to the northeastern Cap Bon Peninsula, give harissa its essence, its strength. Dark and shriveled, smelling of dried fruits, loam, tobacco, smoke, and anise,

the peppers have all the complexities of wine—and some of the heat of fire. The trick is nuanced blending of varieties.

Tunisians are famous for their liberal use of harissa. It's also popular with Algerians, though less so with Moroccans. I have heard more than one Moroccan dismiss it as a substitute for flavor. But good, homemade harissa adds a different dimension of taste, a tangy kick to the dish, and it's easy to see such comments as the rhetoric of culinary rivalry. The best I've sampled was in the Jerban home of Abderrazak Haouari (see page 202); fiery and robust, but flavorful. "The key," he divulged, "is *lots* of garlic." In Morocco, I've tasted brisk, zippy versions, looser, more salsa-like, and flavored with preserved lemons.

## COUSCOUS PRESENTATION

Serving differs across North Africa. Though varying from table to table, Tunisians and Moroccans tend to moisten the couscous grains with some broth, slowly working it in so that it's moist but not mushy. They serve the mounded grains topped with meat or fish, the vegetables scattered around the base, and the remaining broth on the side. Many Algerians pile the couscous into a massive mound and ornately decorate it with strips of carrots, turnips, and small zucchini plus individual chickpeas. The meat is served separately on a platter and the vegetable-laden broth in a tureen to be added as desired. The presentation in these recipes respects each dish's origin.

# Harissa

| | | | | |
|---|---|---|---|---|
| 2 | ounces dried chile peppers (see Note) | | ½ | teaspoon coriander seeds, dry roasted and ground |
| 2 | garlic cloves, peeled | | 1 | teaspoon salt |
| 1 | teaspoon caraway seeds, dry roasted and ground | | ⅓ | cup olive oil plus more for covering |

Wearing rubber gloves, wipe the chile peppers with a damp rag. Stem and seed the peppers and cut into pieces. Soak for 30 minutes in 2 cups of hot water to soften; drain.

Sterilize a 1-pint glass pickling jar in a boiling water bath.

Purée the chile peppers in a blender or pass them through a food mill. Add the garlic, caraway, coriander, salt, and the 1/3 cup olive oil and purée or grind into a smooth paste.

Spoon the mixture into the sterilized jar and cover with a layer of oil.

The harissa will keep up to 1 year in the refrigerator if the paste remains covered with oil.

NOTE: DRIED CHILE PEPPERS FOUND IN LATIN AMERICAN MARKETS WORK WELL FOR HARISSA. *CHORICERO* ARE MILD AND SWEET. FLATTISH *ANCHO* OR *POBLANO* CHILES ARE SIMILAR BUT SLIGHTLY SPICIER. *MULATO* CHILES ARE SMOKY WITH HINTS OF LICORICE. *PASILLA* CHILES ARE NAMED "LITTLE RAISIN" BECAUSE OF THEIR SIMILAR DARK COLOR AND AROMA. USE *GUALLIJO* CHILES FOR AN EARTHY, SPICY BITE, AND TRY *ARBOL* CHILES FOR HEAT. FOR MILDNESS, BLEND IN CALIFORNIA CHILES.

## Couscous Preparation

### Steaming in a couscoussier: the basic method

This method uses water in the bottom of the couscoussier, though for many, but not all, savory couscouses, the pot would be filled with a vegetable- and meat-laden stew. Steaming couscous grains are not covered with a lid. See the note on preparing couscous in these recipes (facing page).

| | | | | |
|---|---|---|---|---|
| 1 | pound couscous (about 2 ½ cups) | | 1 | teaspoon salt |
| 8½ | cups cool water | | 1 | tablespoon butter or smen (optional) |
| 2 | tablespoons extra-virgin olive oil | | | |

Place the couscous in a large, wide bowl and add 8 cups of the water. Swirl and sift with the fingers for 2 to 3 minutes and then drain off the water by cupping a hand against the side of the bowl. Work in 1 tablespoon of the oil with your hands. Let the grains absorb the moisture for 30 minutes. Toss with both hands, lifting the grains and letting them fall through your fingers. Work out any clumps by rubbing your palms together as if warming your hands, letting the grains drop into the bowl.

Fill the bottom part of the couscoussier with about 4 inches of water (and at least 2 inches below the level of the basket), place a strip of aluminum foil around the rim to ensure a good seal between the sections, and bring the water to a boil.

Transfer the couscous to the steaming basket handful by handful, rubbing out any clumps. Place the basket snugly on top of the bottom section of the couscoussier. Steam uncovered for 20 minutes, starting the timing once the steam rises up through the couscous.

Turn the couscous out into the bowl. Break up any larger clumps with a wooden spoon. Let cool for 5 minutes. Slowly sprinkle the remaining $1/2$ cup of water and the salt onto the couscous. Mix well with your hands, again lifting and letting the grains fall through your

fingers. Work in the remaining 1 tablespoon of oil with your hands. Let stand for 5 minutes.

Transfer the grains a handful at a time back to the steaming basket, rubbing them between your palms to work out any clumps, and letting them fall into the basket. Place the basket snugly on top of the bottom section of the couscoussier for a second steaming. Steam uncovered for 25 minutes, starting the counting once the steam rises up through the couscous.

Check the couscous for doneness. The grains should be tender but not mushy. If they have too much bite to them, steam for another 5 minutes. If still not yet tender, turn the grains out into a bowl, break up any larger clumps with a wooden spoon, sprinkle with a bit more cool water, work out any clumps, and return to the top of the couscoussier for a third time, steaming until tender.

Turn the couscous back out into the bowl. Break up any larger clumps with a wooden spoon.

Once the couscous is cool enough to handle, rake through the grains a final time with your fingers, making sure there are no clumps. Work in the smen (if using). Fluff with a fork before piling the grains onto a serving bowl or platter.

## Maximizing precooked "instant" couscous

By ignoring the directions on the box—No boiling water! Not in 5 minutes!—and following the ones below, precooked "instant" couscous can be coaxed into light, fluffy grains.

SERVES 4 TO 6

| | |
|---|---|
| 1 | teaspoon salt |
| 2 ½ | cups warm water |
| 1 | pound couscous (about 2 ½ cups) |

| | |
|---|---|
| 2 | tablespoons extra-virgin olive oil |
| 1 | tablespoon butter or smen (optional) |

Dissolve the salt in the water.

Pour the couscous into a very wide, shallow dish and dribble the warm salty water over it. Mix with a fork. Let sit without disturbing for 10 minutes. Drizzle in the oil. Toss with both hands, lifting the grains and letting them fall through your fingers. Work out any clumps by rubbing your palms together as if warming your hands, letting the grains drop into the dish.

Before serving, preheat the oven to 350°F.

Transfer the couscous to an ovenproof baking dish and bake, turning the grains over from time to time, until steamy warm, 10 to 15 minutes. Work in the smen (if adding). Fluff with a fork before piling the grains onto a serving bowl or platter.

A NOTE ON PREPARING COUSCOUS IN THESE RECIPES:

THE RECIPES IN THIS BOOK CAN BE PREPARED WITH STANDARD COUSCOUS STEAMED IN A COUSCOUSSIER OR THE PRECOOKED "INSTANT" VARIETY PREPARED WITH WATER AND WARMED IN THE OVEN.

IF USING A COUSCOUSSIER, ADD THE INGREDIENTS TO THE STEW AS NEEDED BEFORE OR BETWEEN STEAMINGS, DEPENDING ON HOW LONG THEY NEED TO COOK AS INDICATED IN THE RECIPE DIRECTIONS. THE PROCESS IS FLEXIBLE: IF THE STEW IS NOT YET DONE BUT THE COUSCOUS GRAINS ARE, REMOVE THE GRAINS AND CONTINUE SIMMERING; IF THE STEW IS DONE BUT THE COUSCOUS GRAINS AREN'T, REMOVE ANY DELICATE INGREDIENTS (FISH, CHICKEN, CERTAIN VEGETABLES), ADD MORE WATER TO THE STEW IF NECESSARY, AND CONTINUE STEAMING UNTIL THE GRAINS ARE TENDER.

# COUSCOUS RECIPES

## Haouari's Fava Potage with Mhammas / Potage Mhammas (Jerba, Tunisia)

I had lunch one winter day with Abderrazak Haouari and his family on the southern Tunisian island of Jerba (see page 202). We ate hearty bowls of this legume stew thick with very large-grain couscous called *mhammas* (see page 161). We squeezed lemon over the top and then stirred in some of Haouari's heady, homemade harissa chile paste. Delicious. Here, I have adapted Haouari's recipe from that memorable lunch.

| | | | | |
|---|---|---|---|---|
| 8 | ounces dried chickpeas | | Salt and freshly ground pepper | |
| 4 | ounces small dried peeled and split fava (broad) beans | 8 | ounces fresh spinach leaves, washed and shredded | |
| 12 | cups water | 2 | small carrots, diced | |
| 1 | medium onion, finely chopped | 1 | small turnip (about 4 ounces), diced | |
| 2 | ripe plum tomatoes, cored, seeded, and puréed | 1 | medium potato, peeled and diced | |
| 2 | tablespoons tomato concentrate | 1 | celery stalk, diced | |
| 4 | garlic cloves, minced | 1 | pound large mhammas or peppercorn-size pasta bullets | |
| 3 | tablespoons extra-virgin olive oil | | Harissa (page 165) | |
| 1 | teaspoon fenugreek seeds, briefly dry roasted and ground | 1 | lemon, cut into wedges | |
| 1 | teaspoon caraway seeds, ground | | | |

The night before you wish to serve this dish, rinse the chickpeas and favas. Place in a large pot, cover with abundant water, and soak. When ready to begin cooking, drain and rinse the beans and rinse the pot.

Return the beans to the pot and cover with the 12 cups water. Bring to a boil, skim off any foam that comes to the surface, lower the heat, cover, and gently boil for 1 hour.

Add the onion, tomatoes, tomato concentrate, garlic, oil, fenugreek, and caraway and season with salt and pepper.

Cover and cook for 30 minutes.

Add the spinach, carrots, turnip, potato, and celery, and stir in the mhammas. Cover and cook until the chickpeas and mhammas are tender, 30 to 40 minutes. The consistency should be quite loose; add more water if necessary.

Stir in a small amount of harissa. Taste for seasoning and adjust as needed.

Serve hot in wide bowls with lemon wedges to squeeze over the top and a bowl of harissa to spoon in as desired.

# Fregola with Fresh Wild Mushrooms / Fregola ai funghi (Sardinia, Italy)

Fregola is a Sardinian version of large-grain couscous with one key difference: the grains are toasted in the oven, giving them a nuttier flavor. The most typical preparation is in clam broth, though the earthiness of the fregola combines perfectly fresh wild mushrooms, a sofrito chunky with cured pancetta, and freshly grated pecorino cheese.

| | | | |
|---|---|---|---|
| 6 | tablespoons extra-virgin olive oil | 10 | cups water |
| 1 | medium onion, finely chopped | 1 | pound fregola |
| ½ | stalk celery with leaves, finely chopped | 2 | pounds assorted wild mushrooms (see Note, page 62) |
| ½ | carrot, finely chopped | 2 | garlic cloves, minced |
| 2 | ounces lean cured pancetta, finely chopped | 2 | tablespoons finely chopped fresh flat-leaf parsley |
| 1 | fourteen-ounce can peeled Italian tomatoes, finely chopped, all juices reserved | 1 | ounce freshly grated pecorino, preferably Pecorino Sardo |
| | Salt and freshly ground pepper | | |

Prepare a sofrito. In a large, heavy saucepan or Dutch oven over medium-low heat, heat 3 tablespoons of the oil. Add the onion, and cook until it begins to soften, about 5 minutes. Add the celery, carrot, and pancetta, and cook until the onion is soft and translucent, about 10 minutes. Add the tomatoes and all their juices, season with salt and pepper, and cook for another 15 to 20 minutes, stirring from time to time, until soft and mushy.

Add the water and bring to a boil. Sprinkle in the fregola and cook until the tender, 15 to 18 minutes. The dish should be just moist enough to need a spoon to eat; add water if needed.

Meanwhile, trim and clean the mushrooms and cut into bite-sized pieces. In a large sauté pan or skillet over medium-high heat, heat the remaining 3 tablespoons of oil. Add the mushrooms and garlic and cook until browned.

Gently stir the mushroom and garlic mixture and the parsley into the fregola and cook for 1 to 2 minutes to blend the flavors. Serve in wide bowls topped liberally with the cheese.

# Berkoukès with Chicken / Berkoukès au poulet (Algeria)

Large Algerian couscous called *berkoukès* are traditionally steamed in a couscoussier before being added to finish cooking in the stew. I have given directions for that here, but the grains can be added directly to the simmering stew; add a bit more liquid and give them another 5 minutes or so cooking time. This quite straightforward, hearty recipe is adapted from Mokhtaria Rezki's *Le couscous algérien*.

| | |
|---|---|
| 1 | pound bone-in chicken thighs or legs |
| 1 | medium onion, grated |
| 4 | tablespoons extra-virgin olive oil |
| 2 | tomatoes, halved, seeded, and grated (see page 162) |
| 1 | tablespoon tomato concentrate diluted in 2 tablespoons warm water |
| 1 | garlic clove, minced |
| 2 | pinches sweet paprika (piment doux) |
| 2 | pinches cayenne pepper (piment fort) |
| | Salt and freshly ground pepper |

| | |
|---|---|
| 8 | cups water |
| 1 | pound mixed vegetables, such as freshly shucked peas, fava beans, thin discs of carrots, and 1-inch-long sections of green beans |
| 1 | potato, peeled and diced |
| ½ | cup canned chickpeas, drained and rinsed |
| 10 | ounces berkoukès (see page 161) or small pasta bullets |
| ½ | cup chopped fresh cilantro |
| 1 | lemon, cut into wedges |

Put the chicken and onion in a large pot. Add 2 tablespoons of the oil and swirl until the ingredients are well coated. Cook over medium heat until the chicken is browned and the onion begins to soften, 5 to 8 minutes. Stir in the tomatoes, tomato concentrate, and garlic. Season with the paprika, cayenne pepper, and salt and pepper; cover with the water. Bring to a boil and cook for 30 minutes. Add the mixed vegetables, potato, and chickpeas and cook for another 30 minutes.

Meanwhile, bring an abundant amount of water to a boil in the bottom of a couscoussier or in a large pot. Toss the berkoukès with 1 tablespoon of the oil, coating the grains well. Transfer to the steaming basket. Once the water is boiling, place the basket firmly over the couscoussier. Steam for 15 minutes, starting the counting when the steams rises up through the berkoukès. Tip the berkoukès into the boiling water below, using a spatula to get any pasta that sticks to the sides. Immediately drain the berkoukès, reserving the hot water. Pour the hot water back into the bottom of the couscoussier and return it to a boil. Drizzle the remaining 1 tablespoon of oil over the berkoukès, mixing until thoroughly coated. Place the basket back on top of the couscoussier and steam the berkoukès for a second time for 15 minutes, starting the counting once the steam rises through the surface.

Transfer the berkoukès to the stew and cook, uncovered, until tender, about 10 minutes; though longer if using larger-size berkoukès. Add more liquid if needed to keep it loose and runny. Stir in the cilantro, remove from the heat, and let rest for 5 minutes. Taste for seasoning and adjust as needed.

Serve hot in wide bowls with lemon wedges to squeeze over top.

## Sauceless Couscous with Fresh Peas / Couscous sans sauce aux petits pois (Algiers, Algeria)

Couscous with fresh peas but *sans* sauce—without sauce or broth—is a specialty in Algiers. The peas are steamed separately and then tossed with the prepared grains. It's simple and surprisingly good. Serve with glasses of milk.

| | | | | |
|---|---|---|---|---|
| 1 | pound fine-grain couscous (about 2½ cups) | | Salt | |
| 8 | ounces shelled fresh peas (about 2 cups) | ¼ | cup butter, cut into small pieces | |

If using a couscoussier, prepare the couscous according to the directions on page 166. If using precooked "instant" couscous, prepare it following the directions on page 167.

Meanwhile, steam the peas until tender but not mushy; season with salt when they are about half cooked.

Work the butter into the couscous. Add the peas and toss until mixed. Mound on a serving platter and serve warm.

# Couscous Salad with Fresh Tomatoes, Cilantro, and Lemon
(Northern Morocco)

On the corner of a tiny street running behind La Boqueria market in Barcelona sits Supermercat Rif, a small Moroccan grocery store that sells, among the standard basics, smen, harissa, ras el hanout, and various brands of Moroccan and Algerian pastas and couscous. One day, when I was buying a five-kilogram sack of couscous, the two women who work there explained to me a typical summer salad they make with couscous. It's as lovely as it is simple. The grains of the couscous are surprisingly supple considering they're not steamed, and the only liquid is from washing the grains and the juice of the tomatoes and lemons. It works with precooked "instant" couscous as well. To make it more substantial, scatter cooked chickpeas across the top.

| | | | | |
|---|---|---|---|---|
| 1 | pound medium-grain couscous (about 2 ½ cups) | | 2 | heaping tablespoons finely chopped fresh cilantro |
| 8 | cups water | | 1 | heaping tablespoon finely chopped fresh flat-leaf parsley |
| 5 | ripe medium tomatoes, halved, seeded, and grated (see page 162) | | | Salt and freshly ground pepper |
| | Juice of 2 lemons | | 3 | tablespoons extra-virgin olive oil |

Place the couscous in a large bowl and add the water. Swirl and sift with your fingers for 2 to 3 minutes. Drain and transfer to a large salad bowl.

Add the tomatoes to the couscous along with the lemon juice, cilantro, and parsley. Season with salt and pepper and mix well. Let the mix sit for at least 1 hour for the flavors to blend and the lemon to mellow.

Add the olive oil and fluff just before serving.

## Classic Seven-Vegetable Couscous / Couscous aux sept légumes (Morocco)

Along with the seven different types of vegetables here, there's chickpeas and lamb—a piece of shoulder (or leg) plus a piece of neck fillet. "The neck has little meat but lots of good fat and flavor," Madame Muniga explained when she shared her version of this classic Moroccan and Algerian couscous with me after a lesson in hand-rolling couscous grains from scratch (see facing page). Chicken can be substituted for the lamb; use 2 pounds of skinless bone-in chicken and add it with the carrots, cabbage, and turnips.

| | |
|---|---|
| 1 ½ | pounds couscous (about 4 cups) |
| 1 ½ | pounds bone-in leg or shoulder of lamb |
| 8 | ounces lamb neck, cut into generous chunks |
| 1 | medium onion, quartered |
| 2 | tomatoes, quartered |
| 1 | cup dried chickpeas, soaked overnight and rinsed |
| 1 | teaspoon ground ginger |
| 30 | strands saffron, dry roasted and ground |
| | Salt and freshly ground pepper |
| 10 | sprigs fresh flat-leaf parsley, rinsed |
| 10 | sprigs fresh cilantro, rinsed |

| | |
|---|---|
| 6 | tablespoons extra-virgin olive oil |
| 8 | cups water |
| 2 | carrots, scrubbed and halved lengthwise |
| ¼ | head green cabbage (about 8 ounces) |
| 2 | small turnips (about 8 ounces), peeled and quartered |
| 8 | ounces pumpkin or butternut squash, peeled, seeded, and cut into 1-inch cubes |
| 3 | zucchini, peeled, quartered lengthwise, and then halved crosswise |
| ½ | cup seedless raisins, rinsed |

If steaming the couscous grains in a couscoussier over the stew, begin preparing it according to the directions on page 166. Add ingredients to the stew before and between steamings as required. If using precooked "instant" couscous, prepare it following the directions on page 167.

Put the lamb, onion, tomatoes, chickpeas, ginger, and saffron, with a little salt and pepper, in a large pot or in the bottom of a couscoussier. Fold the parsley and cilantro in half, tie into a tight bundle with cotton kitchen string, and add. Add the oil and swirl until the ingredients are well coated. Cover with the water and bring to a boil. Reduce the heat, partly cover (if using a large pot; if using a couscoussier, cover fully with a steaming basket), and cook at a low boil for 45 minutes. Add the carrots, cabbage, and turnip, and continue to cook for 30 minutes. Add the pumpkin, zucchini, and raisins and cook for a final 30 minutes. There should be at least 4 to 5 cups of broth; stir in water if necessary.

Remove the parsley and cilantro from the stew and discard.

To serve, slowly moisten the couscous grains with 1 cup of broth. Mound the grains in a large serving bowl. Make a wide well in the top. Using a slotted spoon, remove the vegetables, beans, and lamb from the pot and place in the well. Serve the remaining broth on the side.

**Primary Source: Madame Muniga, Marseille, France**

One cold, clear Mediterranean winter afternoon five or six years ago, a French friend and I crossed the central Marseille neighborhood of Belsunce to a wide street near Gare Saint Charles and Madame Muniga's flat.

Madame Muniga was a friend of friends, a retired college Arabic teacher from Morocco who divided her time between here and Casablanca. She had agreed to give me a lesson in the ancient art of hand-rolling couscous from scratch.

Madame Muniga's family comes together for lamb or vegetable couscous every Friday after midday prayers. "That is the day for sharing," she said. She dislikes boxed couscous. "It cooks too fast and sticks together," she said flatly. For these occasions, she prefers to use hand-rolled grains.

In her airy kitchen, under high ceilings detailed in Arabic filigrees and curving niches (her husband was a carpenter), I followed her lead and rolled couscous grains from two sizes of semolina flour and drops of salted water. She spun the flour into little balls in a refined, practiced circular motion with her fingers. We passed the grains through a fine sieve to separate smaller grains from larger ones, which were rerolled until small enough to pass through the sieve as well. I learned what a laborious process it is and understood why many people rarely do it these days; when it is prepared, there's usually a group pitching in and making enough to last a while.

Madame Muniga was a gracious and patient teacher, and as we worked, she talked at length about the tradition of couscous, especially during this time of year: it was the middle Ramadan. The following week she would be taking couscous to the mosque in honor of the Koran. She also offered opinions on regional differences with the dish; comments often tinged with culinary competitiveness.

"Tunisians add harissa because of a lack of flavor and imagination," she said referring to the famed chile paste.

When we finished rolling the couscous, and the last grains had been sifted and set out to dry, Madame Muniga insisted on preparing tea. Her beautiful, rail-thin teenage daughter had just come in from school, and Madame Muniga gave her some coins to go down and buy a bundle of fresh mint.

As Madame Muniga brewed tea, I took notes on her every move. My own attempts at making tea always paled to those I had drunk on my travels across North Africa.

Just as she had been with the couscous, she patiently prepared the tea. It took about fifteen minutes to get it right, pouring scalding liquid back and forth from the pot into a small clear glass, letting the flavors slowly bloom and meld, adjusting the sweetness. When she was—at last!—satisfied, she poured the tea from the pot to a glass and from there into serving glasses with ornate gilded patterns and gold rims.

She set out a plate of sticky, crescent-shaped nut-filled pastries. Being Ramadan, she didn't have any tea or pastries herself, but her mother came into the kitchen for a glass—an elderly figure I had only glimpsed ghosting through the apartment.

My friend and I left not long afterward, walking back through Belsunce. The afternoon was winding down, and people were hustling through the predominately North African neighborhood picking up last-minute provisions for the fast-breaking *iftar* meal. We stopped in one of the many small shops stocked with an assortment of goods—more stacked than displayed—for a square box of the same Chinese gunpowder green tea that Madame Muniga had used.

CONTINUED

The following week, back home in Barcelona, I bought a similar battered teapot and, from a *halal* butcher in the Raval, my first couscoussier along with a few kilograms of couscous that he scooped out of a burlap sack with his blood-stained hands.

I have made dozens, even hundreds, of pots of mint tea since then. The taste is close to what I remember in Marseille that day, though I am still far from rolling couscous with Madame Muniga's agility and ability. Perhaps after a hundred more tries. But I doubt it.

## Mint Tea

In North Africa (and Marseille!) mint tea is generally drunk enormously sweet—the kind of sweetness that makes you a bit thirsty—which is exactly how I like it. Start with ¼ cup of sugar and add more if you want it sweeter. To avoid any bitterness, do not let the tea boil once the mint has been added. For an earthy, Tunisian touch, dry roast a handful of pine nuts and drop then in the glass just before serving.

| | |
|---|---|
| 1 | tablespoon loose-leaf gunpowder green tea |
| 3 | cups plus 3 tablespoons cool water |
| ¼ | to ½ cup sugar |

| | |
|---|---|
| 1 | large handful of fresh mint, rinsed and picked over |
| 4 | tablespoons pine nuts, dry roasted (optional) |

In a stove-top teapot, add the tea leaves and cover with the 3 tablespoons of water. Bring to a quick boil and immediately pour off the water, being carefully that no tea leaves escape. (This gets rid of some of the bitterness, and allows the tea to steep longer with mint.)

Add the sugar to the wet grounds and cover with the remaining 3 cups of water. Over medium heat, with the lid open or off, bring to a boil.

Pour half of the liquid into a bowl or Pyrex measuring cup; reserve. Stuff the mint into the teapot, pressing it against the bottom of the pot with a spoon to gently and slightly crush the leaves. Return the reserved liquid to the teapot.

Simmer over low heat for a few minutes to let the mint infuse. Pour a glassful into a clear drinking glass and then back into the pot, from as high as possible without spilling to aerate the tea and blend the flavors. Repeat this two or three more times, as the color of tea changes from clear to a cloudy caramel.

Begin tasting for sweetness and flavor. Add more sugar if desired, or let it simmer another few minutes to make it stronger. Continue to pour glassfuls in and out of the pot until satisfied with both the sweetness and strength of the tea.

Serve in small clear tea glasses. Do not pour tea into them from the teapot, but from the glass used for mixing and testing (this will help trap any sediment).

If adding pine nuts, sprinkle into the glasses of tea before serving.

# Couscous Lahlou (Kabylie, Alberia)

This typical Algerian Berber couscous with red sauce and plenty of vegetables comes from Restaurant Dar Lahlou in Algiers (facing page), where it's served with both semolina couscous and barley couscous. (See Sources on page 211 for where to find barley couscous.) This is a festive dish, eaten for celebrations and special occasions, but also for midweek dinners like the ones I shared with Sid Ali and his family recently.

| | |
|---|---|
| 1 | pound barley or semolina couscous (about 2 ½ cups) |
| 2 | pounds bone-in lamb shoulder, cut into pieces |
| 1 | medium onion, finely chopped |
| ¼ | teaspoon ground cinnamon |
| | Salt and freshly ground pepper |
| 1 | generous tablespoon extra-virgin olive oil |
| 5 | carrots, scrubbed, halved crosswise, and then halved lengthwise |

| | |
|---|---|
| ½ | cup chickpeas, soaked overnight and rinsed |
| 8 | cups water |
| 8 | ounces green beans, ends trimmed and snapped in half |
| 1 | tomato, halved, seeded, and grated (see page 162) |
| 1 | tablespoon tomato concentrate |
| 4 | small zucchini, scrubbed, halved crosswise, and then halved lengthwise |

If steaming the couscous grains in a couscoussier over the stew, begin preparing it according to the directions on page 166. Add ingredients to the stew before and between steamings as required. If using precooked "instant" couscous, prepare it following the directions on page 167.

Put the lamb, onion, and cinnamon, with some salt and pepper, in a large pot or in the bottom of a couscoussier. Add the oil and swirl until the ingredients are well coated. Cook until the lamb is browned and the onion is soft, 5 to 10 minutes.

Add the carrots and chickpeas and cover with the water. Bring to a boil, reduce the heat, partly cover (if using a large pot; if using a couscoussier, cover fully with a steaming basket), and cook at a gentle boil for 1 hour and 15 minutes.

Add the green beans, tomato, and tomato concentrate and cook, partly covered, for 10 minutes.

Add the zucchini and cook for another 10 minutes or until the vegetables are tender. There should be 3 to 4 cups of broth; stir in water if necessary. Taste the broth for seasoning and adjust as needed.

To serve, mound the couscous in a large ceramic bowl. Transfer the lamb with a slotted spoon to a platter. Decorate the couscous with strips of carrots and zucchini and pattern some of the chickpeas around the sides. Serve the vegetable-laden sauce on the side with the couscous and platter of lamb.

**Primary Source: Sid Ali Lahlou, Algiers, Algeria**

Algiers is a gorgeous Mediterranean capital. Gleaming white buildings trimmed in electric blue rise in tiers above the working port stretching across the city's breadth. On the north side is one of the city's highlights, the kasbah with its tight warren of alleys stretching from the seafront up to the citadel; on the south side is another—the city's best couscous, served at the family-run Restaurant Dar Lahlou.

"The key is working with the hands," Sid Ali Lahlou, a tall, handsome Berber with a few dashing wisps of gray in his jet-black hair, told me in not much more than a whisper this winter. He held up his hands. "The hands!" Between us sat dwindling bowls of red, vegetable-rich broth; a platter of succulent, long-simmered lamb; and two kinds of light, fluffy couscous grains: pale ones made from semolina wheat and nuttier-tasting gray ones from barley.

That hands-on work begins at the family's other enterprise, the Maison Lahlou factory in the mountainous region of Kabylie, about sixty miles east of Algiers, where couscous is hand—not machine—made. As well as the sixty core employees at the factory, there is a network of women working at home that tops 500 during busy summer season as the couscous is dried in the sun— "100 percent organic!" The laborious process involves rolling the grains from two sizes of flour, water, and salt. "It is a spécialité," Sid Ali explained. "People don't have the knowledge anymore—or the time."

A company truck drives around the narrow mountain roads delivering flour and picking up rolled grains. Maison Lahlou produces 504 metric tons of couscous made from semolina wheat and 108 tons from barley each year, as well as some from acorn, corn, and, unusually, rice.

That's more than 600,000 of the one-kilogram sacks! For now it's exported only to France, but Sid Ali hopes to change that soon.

This family venture might be carrying on a dying tradition, but Sid Ali is more proud of providing work to so many women who, otherwise, have few employment opportunities.

He is also spreading his traditional version of Berber couscous. In 2005, he represented Algeria at the world couscous festival in San Vito lo Capo, Sicily, bringing back top prize.

Just as in Berber homes around the country, Dar Lahlou's cook, a Berber named Abri Arezki from Drael Mezant, the same village as the Lahlou clan, patiently moistens the dry grains in a massive, wide-mouthed wooden bowl and rubs them between his palms to work out any lumps before double-steaming them in a large couscoussier. The grains are heaped on a ceramic plate, exquisitely decorated with strips of vegetables and individual chickpeas, and eaten with slender, foot-long wooden spoons.

"Berber handmade," Sid Ali said proudly, as I took another bite. He meant the spoon itself, but he could have been referring to every element of the meal.

Tradition—from beginning to end.

# Lamb Couscous with Meatballs /
# Couscous d'agneau aux boulettes (Tunisia)

My two girls love couscous, though each prefers a different type. My younger daughter, Maia, favors Sicilian-style fish couscous with plenty of broth ladled over top (page 196), while her older sister, Alba, likes this lamb couscous with meatballs. She likes it for the flavor but also perhaps because it's what we always order at Sur le Pouce on our twice-yearly, week-long visits to Marseille.

Little has changed in this hurried, noisy restaurant since a friend first took me there almost a decade ago. I remember so clearly walking down the hill from the train station, through the Belsunce neighborhood to Sur le Pouce, where we crammed around one of the worn, closely set marble tables among mostly North African men, many younger, many alone, to wolf down heaped bowls of inexpensive couscous. I had been in Morocco not long before and was craving good, authentic couscous; here it was: double steamed and waiting to be devoured.

These days it's Alba who devours the couscous with similar speed and pleasure—something I watch with a certain pride.

| | | | | |
|---|---|---|---|---|
| 1 | pound couscous (about 2 ½ cups) | | 1 ½ | cups canned chickpeas, drained and rinsed |
| 2 | pounds bone-in lamb shank, shoulder, or leg, cut into 4 or 5 pieces | | 1 | stalk celery |
| ¾ | teaspoon ground pink peppercorns | | 1 | medium leek (white and tender green parts only), trimmed and cut into 1-inch-thick discs |
| ¾ | teaspoon ground cinnamon | | 1 | zucchini, peeled and cut into 1-inch-thick discs |
| ¾ | teaspoon dried mint | | 20 | sprigs fresh cilantro, rinsed |
| | Salt and freshly ground pepper | | 10 | sprigs fresh flat-leaf parsley, rinsed |
| 4 | tablespoons extra-virgin olive oil | | 1 | pound ground beef or veal |
| 1 ½ | onions, finely chopped | | 1 | large egg, beaten |
| 2 | tablespoons tomato concentrate | | ½ | cup breadcrumbs |
| 1 | carrot, cut into ½-inch-thick discs | | | Oil for frying |
| 1 | small white turnip | | | Flour for dusting |
| 8 | cups water | | | Harissa (see page 165) |

If steaming the couscous grains in a couscoussier over the stew, begin preparing it according to the directions on page 166. Add ingredients to the stew before and between steamings as required. If using precooked "instant" couscous, prepare it following the directions on page 167.

Place the lamb in a large bowl with ½ teaspoon of the pink peppercorns, ½ teaspoon of the cinnamon, and ½ teaspoon of the dried mint, with some salt and pepper. Add 2 tablespoons of the olive oil and swirl to coat the lamb. Cover, refrigerate, and marinate for at least 1 hour.

In a large pot or the bottom of a couscoussier, over medium heat, heat the remaining 2 tablespoons of olive oil. Add the onions and cook until soft, 5 to 10 minutes. Remove one-third of the onions and reserve for the meatballs. Stir in the tomato concentrate, add the carrot and turnip, and the marinated lamb with its marinade. Cover with the water and bring to a boil. Reduce the heat, partly cover (if using a large pot; if using a couscoussier, cover fully with a steaming basket), and cook for 30 minutes.

Add the chickpeas, celery, leek, and zucchini. Fold the cilantro and parsley in half, tie into a tight bundle with cotton kitchen string, and add. Cook for another 30 minutes.

Meanwhile, in a large bowl, add the ground beef, egg, reserved onions, and the remaining ¼ teaspoon of pink peppercorns, ¼ teaspoon of the cinnamon, and ¼ teaspoon of the dried mint, and season with salt and pepper. Begin mixing in the breadcrumbs (there might be some left over) and mix to a smooth consistency. Form about 6 round meatballs.

In a sauté pan or skillet over medium-high, heat about 1 inch deep of the frying oil. Working in batches if necessary, flour the meatballs and fry until golden on each side. Transfer to a plate.

Slide the meatballs into the broth and simmer for a final 30 minutes. Taste the broth for seasoning and adjust as needed.

To serve, transfer the meatballs and pieces of lamb with a slotted spoon to a platter. Remove and discard the celery, turnip, and herbs. Moisten the couscous with 1 cup of broth. Mound the grains on a large serving platter. Scatter the vegetables around the couscous. Serve the remaining broth on the side with the couscous, the platter of meatballs and lamb, and a dish of harissa.

## Lamb Couscous with Pistachios, Almonds, Pine Nuts, and Golden Raisins / Couscous d'agneau aux fruits secs (Tunisia)

This is one of those dishes whose perfection is affixed to a memory: a dinner in Sidi Bou Saïd, the charming white-washed Tunisian village that clings to the cliffs above the azure Mediterranean just up from the ruins of ancient Carthage, on my first night in Tunisia after a year away. Pleasures in the various textures of the dish—the fluffy couscous grains, the nuts and sweet golden raisins, the tender lamb tearing easily off the bone—and in the rich, savory flavors just tinged with sweetness. But perhaps even more, the pleasure in being back.

| | |
|---|---|
| 1 | pound couscous (about 2 ½ cups) |
| 3 | pounds bone-in lamb shoulder or leg, cut into 6 to 8 pieces |
| 8 | ounces neck of lamb |
| | Salt and freshly ground pepper |
| 2 | tablespoons extra-virgin olive oil |
| 1 | large onion, chopped |
| 1 | three-inch piece cinnamon stick |
| 20 | saffron threads, dry roasted and ground |
| 4 | whole cloves |
| ¼ | teaspoonful ground ginger |
| ¼ | teaspoon ground turmeric |

| | |
|---|---|
| 1 ½ | tablespoons tomato concentrate |
| 1 | carrot, scrubbed |
| 1 | turnip, scrubbed |
| 7 | cups water |
| ¼ | cups small golden raisins (*sultanas*) |
| 2 | tablespoons butter |
| ¼ | cup toasted almonds, skins slipped off, some roughly chopped |
| ¼ | cup pine nuts |
| ¼ | cup shelled pistachios |
| | Harissa (page 165) |

If steaming the couscous grains in a couscoussier over the stew, begin preparing it according to the directions on page 166. Add ingredients to the stew before and between steamings required. If using precooked "instant" couscous, prepare it following the directions on page 167.

Generously season the lamb with salt and pepper.

In a large pot or in the bottom of a couscoussier, over medium-high, heat the oil. Add the onion and lamb and cook, stirring frequently, until the lamb is browned and the onion is soft, about 10 minutes.

Add the cinnamon, saffron, cloves, ginger, turmeric, and tomato concentrate; swirl until the lamb is well coated. Add the carrot and turnip and cover with the water. Bring to a boil, reduce the heat, partly cover (if using a large pot; if using a couscoussier, cover fully with a steaming basket), and cook at a gentle boil for 2 hours or until the lamb is very tender but is not falling off the bone.

CONTINUED

Soak the raisins in tepid water for 15 minutes; drain.

In a small saucepan over low heat, melt the butter. Add the almonds, pine nuts, pistachios, and raisins, and cook until the nuts are browned and the raisins plump, about 5 minutes. Transfer to a bowl.

Transfer the lamb and vegetables with a slotted spoon to a platter. Strain the broth, discarding the solids. Taste the broth and adjust the seasoning as needed. Stir some harissa into the broth if desired.

To serve, moisten the couscous with 1 cup of broth. Mound the couscous on a large serving platter. Sprinkle the nuts and raisins over the top and then crown it with the lamb. Serve the remaining broth and a dish of harissa on the side.

## Couscous with Winter Vegetables / Couscous aux legumes d'hiver (Algeria)

Algerian couscouses tend to be hearty, straightforward, and chunky with vegetables. This winter version includes cardoons, a cousin of the artichoke that looks a bit like a hairy, silver-gray celery stalk. But whereas the budding flower of the artichoke is eaten, it's the cardoon's stem that's edible. Chicken or lamb add a depth of flavor here, but, for a vegetarian couscous, simply replace it with more veggies.

| | | | | |
|---|---|---|---|---|
| 1 | pound couscous (about 2 ½ cups) | | 2 | stalks cardoons, tough ends trimmed, thistles stripped away, halved lengthwise, and cut into 2-inch-long pieces |
| 1 | pound bone-in chicken or lamb, cut into 2 or 3 pieces | | ½ | cup dried chickpeas, soaked overnight and rinsed, or ¾ cup canned chickpeas, drained and rinsed |
| 1 | medium onion, grated | | 8 | cups water |
| ¼ | teaspoon ground coriander | | ¼ | head green cabbage |
| 1 | pinch ground cinnamon | | 1 | tomato, halved, seeded, and grated (see page 162) |
| ½ | teaspoon sweet paprika (piment doux) | | 2 | tablespoons tomato concentrate |
| ¼ | teaspoon cayenne pepper (piment fort) | | 8 | ounces acorn, butternut, or another winter squash, rind removed and cut into 1-inch cubes |
| | Salt and freshly ground pepper | | 10 | ounces fresh fava beans, shucked (about ½ cup shucked favas) |
| 1 | tablespoon olive oil | | | |
| 2 | carrots, scrubbed, halved crosswise, and then halved lengthwise | | | |
| 2 | turnips (about 10 ounces), scrubbed and quartered lengthwise | | | |

If steaming the couscous grains in a couscoussier over the stew, begin preparing it according to the directions on page 166. Add ingredients to the stew before and between steamings as required. If using precooked "instant" couscous, prepare it following the directions on page 167.

Put the chicken, onion, coriander, cinnamon, paprika, and cayenne pepper, with some salt and pepper, in a large pot or in the bottom of a couscoussier. Add the oil and swirl until the ingredients are well coated. Cook over medium heat until the chicken is browned and the onion begins to soften, about 5 minutes.

Add the carrots, turnips, cardoons, and chickpeas (if dried), cover with the water, and bring to a boil. Reduce heat, partly cover (if using a large pot; if using a couscoussier, cover fully with a steaming basket), and cook at a low boil for 30 minutes. Add the cabbage, tomato, and tomato concentrate and cook for another 30 minutes. Add the squash and fava beans, (and, if using canned chickpeas, add them here) and cook for a final 30 minutes. There should be about at least 4 cups of broth; stir in water if necessary. Taste for seasoning and adjust as needed.

To serve, mound the couscous on a large serving dish. Transfer the chicken with a slotted spoon to a platter. Decorate the couscous with half of the vegetables. Serve the vegetable-laden sauce on the side with the couscous and chicken.

# Couscous with Chicken, Caramelized Onions, and Raisins / Couscous de poulet aux oignons confits et raisins secs (Morocco)

Another great Moroccan chicken couscous, this one exemplifies culinary sophistication and the perfect blending of sweet and savory. The key is the caramelized onion and raisin mix, known as *tfaya*. Be patient, allowing almost two hours for this. It's worth it.

| | | | |
|---|---|---|---|
| 1 | pound fine-grain couscous (about 2 ½ cups) | 1 | stalk celery, folded in half |
| 5 | tablespoons extra-virgin olive oil | 1 | carrot, halved |
| 2 | pounds red onions, cut into thin slices | 1 | turnip, halved |
| ⅓ | cup sugar | 10 | sprigs fresh cilantro, rinsed |
| ½ | cup raisins | 10 | sprigs fresh flat-leaf parsley, rinsed |
| 4 | pounds bone-in chicken thighs and legs, skin pulled off | 5 | cups water |
| 1 | three-inch piece cinnamon stick | | Salt and freshly ground pepper |
| ½ | teaspoonful ground ginger | ¾ | cup whole toasted almonds, skins slipped off |
| 20 | saffron threads, dry roasted and ground | 3 | hard-boiled eggs, peeled and halved |
| 4 | cloves | | |

If steaming the couscous grains in a couscoussier over the stew, begin preparing it according to the directions on page 166. Add ingredients to the stew before and between steamings as required. If using precooked "instant" couscous, prepare it following the directions on page 167.

In a heavy sauté pan or skillet, heat 4 tablespoons of the oil. Add the onions and sugar, cover snugly with a lid, and cook very slowly over low heat for 1 hour, stirring from time to time. Remove the lid and cook uncovered until the liquid has evaporated and the onions are golden, 30 to 45 minutes.

Meanwhile, soak the raisins in tepid water for 15 minutes; drain.

When the onions are golden, scatter the raisins over them and cook for a final 10 minutes or so until the onions are caramelized.

Meanwhile, put the chicken, cinnamon stick, ginger, saffron, and cloves in a large pot or in the bottom of a couscoussier. Add the remaining 1 tablespoon of oil and swirl until the ingredients are well coated. Add the celery, carrot, and turnip. Fold the cilantro and parsley together, tie into a tight bundle with cotton kitchen string, and add. Cover with the water, bring to a boil, and

CONTINUED

skim off any foam that comes to the surface. Season the broth with salt and pepper, reduce the heat, partly cover (if using a large pot; if using a couscoussier, cover fully with a steaming basket), and cook until the chicken is tender but not falling off the bone, about 40 minutes.

Transfer the chicken pieces with a slotted spoon to a platter. Strain the broth into a bowl, discarding the vegetables, herbs, and cinnamon stick. Taste for seasoning and adjust as needed.

To serve, moisten the couscous with $1/2$ cup of broth. Mound the couscous on a large serving platter or dish. Make a wide well in the top and place the pieces of chicken in the middle. Spread the onion-and-raisin mixture around the mound and sprinkle the almonds over the top. Garnish with the hard-boiled eggs and serve with the remaining broth on the side.

# Couscous with Fresh Fava Beans and Chicken / Couscous aux fèves fraîches et au poulet (Algeria)

The mountainous Kabylie region east of Algiers is Berber and couscous heartland. Couscous's prominent role is clear in local cookbooks. Take Madame Bouhamed's *Cuisine Kabyle*: twenty-three out of the thirty-seven savory recipes are for couscous or its larger cousin, berkoukès. This recipe is adapted from one of the many lovely, simple, and delicious dishes she includes.

| | | | | |
|---|---|---|---|---|
| 1 | whole chicken (about 4 pounds) | | 3 | tablespoons extra-virgin olive oil |
| 1 | medium onion, cut into very thin slices | | 1 | pound couscous (about 2 ½ cups) |
| 1 | garlic clove, minced | | 5 | cups water |
| ¼ | teaspoon sweet paprika (piment doux) | | 2 | tomatoes, halved, seeded, and grated (see page 162) |
| ¼ | teaspoon or cayenne pepper (piment fort) | | 1 | tablespoon tomato concentrate |
| 1 | teaspoon ground coriander seeds | | 2 | pounds fresh fava beans, shelled (about 2 ½ cups shucked favas) (see Note) |
| | Salt and freshly ground pepper | | | |

Clean the chicken and trim any excess fat. Cut into about 8 pieces. Wash well and pat dry with paper towels.

Place the chicken pieces in a large glass bowl with the onion, garlic, paprika, cayenne pepper, and coriander, with some salt and pepper. Add the oil and swirl until the chicken is well coated. Cover, refrigerate, and marinate for at least 1 hour.

If steaming the couscous grains in a couscoussier over the stew, begin preparing it according to the directions on page 166. Add ingredients to the stew before and between steamings as required. If using precooked "instant" couscous, prepare it following the directions on page 167.

In a large pot or in the bottom of a couscoussier, bring the water to a boil. Add the chicken with its marinade, the tomatoes, and tomato concentrate, and return to a boil. Reduce the heat, partly cover (if using a large pot; if using a couscoussier, cover fully with a steaming basket), and simmer for 45 minutes. Add the fava beans and cook for another 15 minutes. The chicken should be very tender but not falling off the bone. There should be at least 4 cups of broth; stir in water if necessary. Taste the broth for seasoning and adjust as needed.

To serve, mound the couscous in a large serving bowl. Transfer the chicken with a slotted spoon to a platter. Decorate the couscous with some of the fava beans. Serve the fava-laden sauce on the side with the couscous and chicken.

NOTE: AS AN ALTERNATIVE TO SHUCKING FAVAS, WHOLE PODS CAN BE CUT INTO 1-INCH-LONG SEGMENTS, BLANCHED, AND THEN ADDED TO THE STEW.

SERVES 6

## Braised Chicken Buried in Sweet Couscous / Couscous sucré au poulet (Tangier, Morocco)

Also known as *seffa bel djedj*, this is another great Moroccan chicken couscous. The origin of this recipe is Tangier and comes from Sanae Nouali, the Moroccan nanny and cook of close friends of ours in Barcelona. The braised chicken is completely buried under sweetened couscous dusted in confectioners' sugar and cinnamon and decorated with almonds. Sanae also prepares it with short pasta noodles instead of couscous (see Sweet Vermicelli, page 154). Both ways are spectacular.

| | | | | |
|---|---|---|---|---|
| 2 | pounds medium-grain couscous (about 5 cups) | ½ | tablespoon salt |
| 1 | whole chicken (about 4 pounds) | ½ | tablespoon freshly ground pepper |
| 2 | large red onions, 1 grated and 1 chopped | 2 | tablespoons butter or smen |
| ⅓ | cup finely chopped fresh flat-leaf parsley | 2 | cups water, plus more as needed |
| 1 | teaspoon ground cinnamon, plus more for dusting | ½ | cup raisins |
| 20 | saffron threads, dry roasted and ground | | Confectioners' sugar for dusting |
| ½ | tablespoon ground ginger | 3 | ounces toasted almonds, skins slipped off |

If steaming the couscous grains in a couscoussier over the chicken, begin preparing it according to the directions on page 166. If using precooked "instant" couscous, prepare it following the directions on page 167.

Clean the chicken. Wash the outside of the chicken and its cavity and pat dry with paper towels. Clip off the fatty "tail" and trim any excess fat that can be reached without tearing the skin.

In a medium bowl, combine the grated onion, the parsley, the 1 teaspoon cinnamon, the saffron, ginger, salt, and pepper. Rub the chicken with the mixture, pushing some gently under the edges of the skin.

Place the chicken, breast-side down, in the bottom of a couscoussier or in a large pot. Spoon over the remaining spiced onion mixture and add the chopped onion and the butter. Cook over medium heat for 15 minutes.

Add 1 cup of the water, swirl, and bring to a boil. Reduce the heat, partly cover (if using a large pot; if using a couscoussier, cover fully with a steaming basket), and cook for 1½ hours until the chicken is very tender but not falling apart. Add in a bit more water if necessary. Turn the chicken breast-side up about 30 minutes into cooking.

Soak the raisins in tepid water for 15 minutes; drain. Mix the raisins into the couscous for the second steaming if using a couscoussier or, if using precooked "instant" couscous, mix the raisins in at the end.

Preheat the oven to 350°F.

Gently lift the chicken whole out of the couscoussier and place on a baking tray. Bake in the oven until the skin is golden brown, about 15 minutes.

Meanwhile, add the remaining 1 cup of water to the couscoussier and bring to a boil. Skim off ¹/₂ cup of liquid and moisten the couscous grains.

Place the chicken in the center of a large serving platter and completely bury it under a mound of couscous. Sprinkle with the confectioners' sugar and draw a pattern of lines with cinnamon. Arrange the almonds across the mound in a decorative fashion.

Serve with the remaining broth on the side with a bowl of confectioners' sugar to further sweeten the couscous if desired.

# Fez-Style Chicken Stuffed with Couscous and Almonds / Poulet farci à la Fassi (Fez, Morocco)

In 1958, Madame Z. Guinaudeau published a cookbook in Rabat called *Fès vu par sa cuisine* (a decade later it was published in English). The wife of a French physician, she lived in Fez for more than thirty years and meticulously documented the city's legendary culinary culture. Included in the book are both sweet and savory versions of the great Andalusian-inspired dish of chicken stuffed with almond-and-raisin-studded couscous. This recipe is an adaptation—and slight modernizing—of the savory one (the recipe begins: "Having slaughtered, plucked, drawn, and washed the chicken according to the caïda or tradition . . . "). I have also increased the amount of couscous. She calls for just a cup so that it fits into the cavity of the bird. That's fine if you are eating a banquet of such succulent dishes, but in our house we don't want anything else besides more of this!

| | | | | |
|---|---|---|---|---|
| 1 | pound couscous (about 2 ½ cups) | | | Ras el hanout (see page 210) |
| 1 | whole chicken (about 4 pounds) | | 2 | medium red onions, chopped |
| | Salt and freshly ground pepper | | | Ground ginger |
| 1 ½ | ounces almonds, skins slipped off, and coarsely chopped | | 10 | saffron threads, dry roasted and ground |
| 1 ½ | ounces seedless raisins, coarsely chopped | | 5 | cups water |
| 2 | tablespoons butter, at room temperature | | | |

If using a couscoussier, prepare the couscous according to the directions on page 166. If using precooked "instant" couscous, prepare it following the directions on page 167.

Clean the chicken and trim any excess fat. Wash the outside of the chicken and its cavity, patting dry with paper towels. Season the cavity with salt and pepper.

Mix 1 cup of the steamed couscous together with the almonds, raisins, 1 tablespoon of the butter, and a pinch of ras el hanout. Loosely stuff the mixture into the chicken. Secure the cavity closed with toothpicks and then truss the legs.

In a stewing pan or Dutch oven that comfortably holds the chicken, add the onions, 2 pinches of ras el hanout, ginger, the saffron, and a pinch of salt. Set the chicken, breast-side down, in the pan and pour the water around it. Bring the water to a boil, add the remaining 1 tablespoon of butter, and cook, partly covered, at a low, steady boil until the meat comes easily off the bone, the liquid has evaporated, and the couscous stuffing is at least 165°F, about 2 hours. Turn the chicken breast-side up about halfway through cooking. Add more water if needed. The onions should be meltingly soft and very moist at the end.

Serve the chicken on a large platter surrounded by the onions with plenty of bread and the remaining couscous.

# Sicilian Couscous with Fish Broth / Cuscus con brodo di pesce (Trapani, Sicily, Italy)

Sicily has its own ancient couscous traditions, and the island's version is distinct from North African ones. To start with, it's made with fish. Or specifically, fish broth. The couscous grains are steamed over water and then soaked in the broth for an hour or so. The dominant spices are cinnamon and bay leaves—some cooks even line the basket of the couscous steamer with bay leaves.

The best I've had was in Trapani at the excellent Slow Food–affiliated Cantina Siciliana. The well-flavored grains are topped with a handful of *calamari fritti*—floured and just-fried calamari—offering a perfect counterpoint in texture.

| | | | | |
|---|---|---|---|---|
| 1 | pound couscous (about 2 ½ cups) | | 2 | tablespoons tomato concentrate |
| 3 | tablespoons extra-virgin olive oil | | 1 | tablespoon roughly chopped fresh flat-leaf parsley |
| 1 | medium onion, finely chopped | | 1 | three-inch piece cinnamon stick, slightly crushed |
| 2 | garlic cloves, minced | | 2 | bay leaves |
| | Peperoncino or red pepper flakes | | | Salt and freshly ground pepper |
| 4 | plum tomatoes, peeled, seeded, and finely chopped | | 7 | cups water |
| 1 | stalk celery, finely chopped | | | |
| 2 ½ | pounds soup fish, such as scorpion fish, roosterfish, grouper, or another firm-fleshed white fish | | | |

If using a couscoussier, prepare the couscous according to the directions on page 166. If using precooked "instant" couscous, prepare it following the directions on page 167.

Meanwhile, in a large pot or Dutch oven over medium-low heat, heat the oil. Add the onion and cook until it begins to soften, about 5 minutes. Add the garlic and some pinches of peperoncino and cook until the onion is translucent and the garlic golden, about 5 minutes. Add the tomatoes and celery and cook, stirring frequently, until they are soft and mushy, about 20 minutes. Lay in the fish and stir to cover with the sauce. Add the tomato concentrate, parsley, cinnamon, and bay leaves and season with salt and pepper. Cover with the water, bring to a boil, reduce the heat, and simmer uncovered for 30 minutes.

Strain the stock through a sieve, pressing out all of the juices. Discard the solids and transfer the broth to a clean saucepan. There should be 4 to 5 cups of broth; stir in water if necessary. Taste for seasoning and adjust as needed. Cover and keep warm.

Place the couscous in a large, wide serving bowl. Pour 3 cups of the broth over it, stir with a fork, and cover tightly with aluminum foil. Wrap in a kitchen towel and let stand for 30 minutes to 1 hour.

Just before serving, fluff the grains. Reheat the remaining broth and serve on the side.

SERVES 6

# Fish Couscous with White Sauce /
# Couscous au poisson en sauce blanche (Algeria)

Although most Algerian couscouses have broths tinted red from fresh tomatoes and tomato concentrate, excellent "white" ones are found along the Mediterranean coast, where they are prepared with freshly caught fish. Grouper is a favorite, though in Algiers I immensely enjoyed the couscous with meaty, almost sweet swordfish steaks.

| | |
|---|---|
| 1 | pound couscous (about 2 ½ cups) |
| 1 | medium onion, finely chopped |
| 2 | garlic cloves, minced |
| 2 | pinches ground cinnamon |
| | Salt and freshly ground pepper |
| 1 | tablespoon extra-virgin olive oil |
| 2 | carrots, scrubbed, halved crosswise, and then halved lengthwise |
| 2 | small turnips, scrubbed, halved crosswise, and then halved lengthwise |

| | |
|---|---|
| ½ | cup chickpeas, soaked overnight and rinsed |
| 7 | cups water |
| 2 | white rose potatoes, peeled and quartered |
| 4 | small zucchini, scrubbed, cut crosswise, and then halved lengthwise |
| 6 | one-inch-thick steaks grouper, swordfish, hake, or another firm-fleshed white fish (2 to 2 ½ pounds) |

If steaming the couscous grains in a couscoussier over the stew, begin preparing it according to the directions on page 166. Add ingredients to the stew before and between steamings as required. If using precooked "instant" couscous, prepare it following the directions on page 167.

Put the onion, garlic, and cinnamon, with some salt and pepper, in a large pot or in the bottom of a couscoussier. Add the oil and swirl until the ingredients are well coated. Cook over medium heat until the onion begins to soften, about 5 minutes.

Add the carrots, turnips, and chickpeas and cover with the water. Bring to a boil, reduce the heat, partly cover (if using a large pot; if using a couscoussier, cover fully with steaming basket), and cook at a low boil for 1 hour. Add the potatoes and cook for 15 minutes. Add the zucchini

and continue cooking for 10 minutes. Gently lay in the fish steaks and cook for a final 20 minutes, swirling from time to time to moisten the top steaks. Taste the broth for seasoning and adjust as needed.

Very carefully transfer the fish with a slotted spoon to a platter without breaking the pieces.

To serve, mound the couscous in a large serving bowl. Decorate the couscous with some of the vegetables and chickpeas. Serve the vegetable-laden sauce in a separate bowl on the side with the couscous and fish.

# Pantellerian Fish Couscous / Cuscus alla pantesca (Pantelleria, Italy)

I tend to travel light and don't buy much in the way of souvenirs when I am on the road, just certain local foodstuffs—mastic in Turkey, barley couscous in Algeria, spice mixes in Morocco—and locally published cookbooks. This recipe is adapted from one of my favorites, Giacomo Pilati and Alba Allotta's *Cucina trapanese e delle isole* (*The Cooking of Trapani and the Islands*).

One of those islands is Pantelleria, laying sixty-three miles southwest of Sicily (and twenty-five miles from Tunisia). A mere three miles across, rimmed in rocky, black coastline, and producing the best capers in the entire Mediterranean, the island offers its own stunning version of fish couscous. The grains are soaked in fish broth just as in Sicily, but then they're topped with the pieces of fish as well as a lush sauté of eggplant, zucchini, and peppers.

| | |
|---|---|
| 1 | pound couscous (about 2 ½ cups) |
| 1 | stalk celery with leaves, roughly chopped |
| 1 | carrot, scrubbed and roughly chopped |
| 1 | bunch fresh flat-leaf parsley |
| 1 | bay leaf |
| 1 | medium onion, finely chopped |
| 12 | tablespoons extra-virgin olive oil |
| 3 | pounds mixed soup fish, such as scorpion fish, rooster-fish, grouper, or another firm-fleshed white fish |
| 2 | garlic cloves, peeled |

| | |
|---|---|
| ½ | cup tomato sauce (*salsa di pomodoro*) or puréed canned, peeled Italian tomatoes |
| | Salt and freshly ground pepper |
| | Peperoncino or red pepper flakes |
| 8 | cups hot water |
| 1 | eggplant, stemmed, washed, and cubed |
| 2 | green zucchini, stemmed, scrubbed, and cubed |
| 2 | fresh Italian peppers or 1 red bell pepper, stemmed, seeded, and cut into ½-inch pieces |

If steaming the couscous grains in a couscoussier, prepare it according to the directions on page 166 with this addition—place the celery, carrot, parsley, bay leaf, and $^1/_2$ of the onion in the bottom of the couscoussier before the steaming.

If using precooked "instant" couscous, prepare it following the directions on page 167 with this addition—bring 3 cups of water to a boil, add the celery, carrot, parsley, bay leaf, and $^1/_2$ of the onion, and simmer for 5 minutes. Remove from the heat and let infuse while it

cools until just warm. Strain, discard the solids, and use the liquid to prepare the couscous.

Meanwhile, in a large pot or Dutch oven over medium heat, heat 6 tablespoons of the oil. Add the fish and fry until golden, turning carefully just once. Transfer with a slotted spoon to a platter.

In the same oil, begin preparing a sofrito. Add the remaining $^1/_2$ of onion and the garlic and cook until the onion begins to soften and the garlic is golden, about 5 minutes. Remove the garlic and discard. Stir in the tomato sauce and season with salt, pepper, and a pinch of peperoncino. Cover with the hot water, bring to a boil, and boil for 10 minutes. Return the fish (and any drippings) to the pot, carefully laying them in the broth. Reduce the heat to low, cover, and gently simmer for 20 minutes. Remove the fish with a slotted spoon and transfer to a platter to cool.

Meanwhile, in a large sauté pan or skillet over medium heat, heat the remaining 6 tablespoons of oil. Fry the eggplant, zucchini, and fresh peppers until soft and golden. Remove with a slotted spoon and lay out on a paper towel–lined plate to drain.

Strain the broth into a clean saucepan; there should be at least 6 cups. Taste for seasoning and adjust as needed. Cover and keep warm. Debone the fish, breaking the fillets into bite-sized pieces.

Place the couscous in a large serving dish. Cover with the vegetables and fish, and then slowly pour over about 4 cups of broth. Mix carefully, cover, and let rest for 1 hour.

Just before serving, gently fluff with a fork. Reheat the remaining broth and serve on the side.

# Tunisian Fish Couscous with Quince / Couscous au poisson et au coing (Tunisia)

Slowly drifting down Tunisia's eight-hundred-mile, Z-shaped coastline is one of the great pleasures of traveling in the country. I love to feel the pace slow and the horizon stretch out as it changes from the green and fertile north, with its European softness, to the desert south that nudges the Sahara.

But there is one constant along the coast: fish couscous. The two best places to eat it are at the top (Dar El Jeld in Tunis) and the bottom (Chef Haouari's in Jerba) of the coast. In winter, both add quince and raisins. This is a Jewish influence dating back to their expulsion from Spain in the 15th century, Tunisian food expert Abderrazak Haouari explained to me one winter evening in Jerba over his version of the dish. "They brought from Andalucía the tradition of mixing fish and fruit, something not found in Tunisian or Berber cooking." (See page 202.)

Dar El Jeld is located in Tunis's ancient medina. There's no sign, just a massive studded yellow door. But inside—ornate, detailed stucco and tile of what was a wealthy 18th-century merchant's home, now tastefully converted by the family into a restaurant. Serving the highest level of traditional Tunisian cuisine, the kitchen, led by the grand-mother, is staffed by only women—perhaps the only place of its kind in Tunisia.

Because there are elements of each restaurant's version of this dish that I love, I drew on those to make my own delicious third version.

| | | | |
|---|---|---|---|
| 1 | pound couscous (about 2 ½ cups) | 1 | tablespoon tomato concentrate |
| 3 | pounds bream, sea bass, or grouper, cut into 4 steaks, or 2 pounds fillets cut into 4 portions | | Harissa (see page 165) |
| | | 2 | tablespoons plus 7 cups water |
| | Salt and freshly ground pepper | 1 | quince, peeled, seeded, and quartered |
| 1 | teaspoon ground cumin | 4 | Italian green peppers, stemmed, seeded, and halved lengthwise, or 2 green bell peppers, stemmed, seeded, and quartered lengthwise |
| 3 | garlic cloves, minced | | |
| 4 | tablespoons extra-virgin olive oil | | |
| 5 | onions, 1 medium, finely chopped and 4 medium-small, peeled | 20 | strands saffron, dry roasted and ground |
| | | ⅔ | cup seedless raisins (3 ounces) |
| 4 | tomatoes, peeled, seeded, and puréed | 1 | cup canned chickpeas, drained and rinsed |

If steaming the couscous grains in a couscoussier over the stew, begin preparing it according to the directions on page 166. Add ingredients to the stew before and between steamings as required. If using precooked "instant" couscous, prepare it following the directions on page 167.

Liberally season the fish with salt and pepper and rub $1/2$ teaspoon of the cumin and half of the garlic into the steaks. Set aside.

In a large pot or in the bottom of a couscoussier, over medium-low heat, heat the oil. Add the chopped onion and cook until it begins to soften, about 5 minutes. Add the tomatoes, tomato concentrate, a bit of harissa, the remaining $1/2$ teaspoon of cumin, and the remaining garlic and season with salt. Add the 2 tablespoons of water, swirl to mix, and cook for 10 minutes until the mixture darkens and loses its acidity.

Add the whole onions, quince, green peppers, and saffron. Swirl to coat and then cover with the remaining 7 cups of water. Bring to a boil, lower the heat, partly cover (if using a large pot; if using a couscoussier, cover fully with a steaming basket), and cook for 30 minutes.

Meanwhile, soak the raisins in a bowl of tepid water for 15 minutes; drain.

Add the chickpeas and raisins to the broth and cook for 30 minutes. Gently lay in the fish and cook for a final 5 to 15 minutes depending on the fish, swirling from time to time to moisten with broth.

Very carefully transfer the fish with a slotted spoon to a platter without breaking the pieces. Strain the broth, reserving the quince, green peppers, chickpeas, and raisins, and discarding the rest of the solids. Taste the broth for seasoning and adjust as needed.

To serve, slowly moisten the couscous with 1 cup of broth. Mound couscous in a large serving bowl. Make a well in the top and place the pieces of fish in the center. Surround the fish with the quince, green peppers, chickpeas, and raisins. Serve the remaining broth on the side with a bowl of harissa to add as desired.

**Primary Source: Abderrazak Haouari, Jerba, Tunisia**

Tethered to Tunisia's southeastern coast by a four-mile-long Roman-built causeway, Jerba is a flat, sun-chafed expanse of the Sahara. But, with a network of underground wells and moist March-to-October sea breezes, the small, 197-square-mile island is fertile, cultivated with a million date palms, 600,000 olive trees, pomegranates, sweet grapes used for raisins, figs, grenadines, and apricots. Scattered among the orchards are fortified farmhouses called *manzels* and hundreds of smooth whitewashed mosques with square-topped minarets.

On my first trip to Jerba a few years ago, I had a single name scribbled in my notebook: Chef Abderrazak Haouari. No address, no phone number, not even a city. It took two days to track him down. At last, rather late in the evening, a battered Peugeot taxi dropped me off in the sandy lot of a tiny, nondescript restaurant opposite a string of European beach resort hotels about twenty minutes south of the island's capital, Houmt Souk.

"Chef Haouari?" I asked a man standing at the door. He greeted me warmly, his eyes disappearing with a smile. The evening was cool, and he wore a long, open-necked woolen robe over a sweater. His eighteen-year-old son, Adel, emerged from the kitchen, a dazzling, infectious smile lighting up his face. "Tea?"

Gentle and warm hearted, Abderrazak Haouari is the country's preeminent culinary authority. After decades of working at the best restaurants in Paris and Brussels, he settled back home and opened a simple restaurant that serves a handful of inexpensive, perfectly executed Tunisian and Jerban dishes: *salade méchouia* (cold puréed roasted peppers, tomatoes, and onions), *ojjas* (scrambled-egg dishes), *briks* (triangular deep-fried puff pastries filled with, among other things, a runny egg), and various couscouses prepared in the island's unique three-tiered couscoussier.

I chatted with Haouari while Adel went into the kitchen to prepare fish couscous with quince for me. The couscous came gently moistened with the tomato-based broth, giving it a reddish tint. The grains were light and fluffy; the flavors balanced. Adel clearly had picked up his father's deft touch.

The following winter, I returned to Jerba and drove directly to Restaurant Chef Haouari for dinner. Father and son offered me tea and then withdrew into the kitchen. Haouari shortly reemerged with a large plate of *seiches sautées*, a familiar Mediterranean dish of tender cuttlefish sautéed in olive oil and garlic but with the distinct Tunisian accent of cumin. A heaped mound of couscous covered in lamb, chickpeas, and vegetables came next. The grains were just as moist and fluffy as I remembered, and the lamb, eaten by hand, succulent.

The olive harvest was in full swing, and I spent almost a week wandering aimlessly in my rental car—a small transistor on the dashboard, playing swooning love songs from Naples on the only station it could receive—stopping to chat with those I came across in the olive fields. For lunch or for dinner, I often saw Haouari, sometimes at the restaurant, sometimes at his house.

On my last Sunday, I returned to the family home for a lively, chatty lunch. Haouari was at the restaurant with Adel, but his other two sons, two daughters, mother-in-law, and wife were home. His wife wore a beautiful embroidered denim gown and apron, a scarf that covered her hair and chin, and a short-brimmed straw hat.

We were eating a green salad assembled from their garden when a truck came bumping down the long, sandy drive. The olive oil man! Everyone rushed outside. A man unloaded two large drums filled with oil cold-pressed from the family's own olives that they had picked just weeks before. A seal was quickly broken, pinkies dipped in, the oil tasted. The youngest boy fetched a white bowl and a small amount was tipped into it. It was cloudy green, full-bodied. The mother-in-law pronounced it excellent. We brought the bowl back inside and spooned the fresh oil onto our salads.

A tomato-rich couscous with mullet followed. We devoured the couscous grains first and then the boney fish, using our fingers. After plump oranges from the garden, we moved to the sitting room for immense, four-inch-long "gazelle's horns," heavy with crushed almonds and honey, and, of course, tea.

The afternoon dissipated, and before I knew it we were back around the table eating a dinner of grilled, cumin- and turmeric-rubbed red mullet, bream, and sea bass.

It was late when I finally slipped away, stopping by the restaurant to say good-bye to Haouari and Adel. They greeted me affectionately. "Tea?"

# Sweet Couscous with Dates and Nuts /
# Couscous sucré aux dattes et fruits secs (Tunisia)

This sweet couscous is a perfect part of a predawn Ramadan meal, filling enough to help carry the faithful through the day's fast until sunset. We love it at home as an afternoon snack. Serve with glasses of cold milk.

| | |
|---|---|
| 1 | pound couscous (about 2 ½ cups) |
| 1 | cup water |
| 1 ½ | cups sugar |
| ½ | cup whole toasted almonds, skins slipped off |
| ½ | cup shelled pistachios |

| | |
|---|---|
| 1 | cup Deglet Noor dates, pitted and halved lengthwise |
| | Orange blossom water |
| | Ground cinnamon for dusting |
| | Confectioners' sugar for dusting |

If using a couscoussier, prepare the couscous according to the directions on page 166. If using precooked "instant" couscous, prepare it following the directions on page 167.

In a small saucepan over high heat, combine the water and the sugar. Bring to a boil, stirring to dissolve the sugar. Remove from the heat and set aside to cool until just warm.

In a small sauté pan or skillet, gently dry-roast the almonds over low heat until warm and fragrant. Coarsely grind half of the almonds and half of the pistachios in a food processor; reserve the remaining almonds and pistachios whole for decoration. Cube half of the dates; set aside the remainder for decoration.

Transfer the couscous to a large bowl. Sprinkle the grains with ½ teaspoon of orange blossom water or to taste, add the ground nuts and date cubes, and blend thoroughly with your hands. Slowly drizzle half of the syrup over the couscous, using your hands to work it in. The couscous should be moist but not soggy.

To serve, mound the grains on a large serving platter. Dust with cinnamon and confectioners' sugar and then decorate with the reserved whole nuts and date halves. Serve the remaining syrup in a small pitcher on the side for those who want their couscous sweeter.

## Sweet Couscous with Raisins / Couscous sucré aux raisins secs (Algeria)

This is a simple sweet couscous, one found across the Maghreb. In Algeria it's known as *seffa b'z-zbib* as well as *mesfouf*. Serve with glasses of cold milk.

| | |
|---|---|
| ½ | cup seedless raisins |
| 8 | ounces fine-grain couscous (about 1 ¼ cups) |
| 2 | tablespoons butter, cut into small pieces |

| | |
|---|---|
| | Confectioners' sugar |
| | Ground cinnamon for dusting |
| 2 | hard-boiled eggs, peeled and halved lengthwise |

Soak the raisins in tepid water for 15 minutes; drain.

If using a couscoussier, prepare the couscous according to the directions on page 166 with this addition—mix the raisins into the couscous for the final steaming.

If using precooked "instant" couscous, prepare it following the directions on page 167 with this addition—mix the raisins into the couscous before warming the grains in the oven.

Transfer the couscous to a large bowl. Work in the butter and liberally sweeten with sugar. Fluff the grains with a fork.

To serve, mound the couscous on a large serving platter. Dust with cinnamon and garnish with the hard-boiled eggs.

## Sweet Couscous in Milk / Couscous sucré au lait (Morocco)

This is a very quick Moroccan dinner dish commonly prepared with leftover couscous. It also makes an excellent snack, especially on one of those typically cold and damp North African winter afternoons. Fine-grain couscous works here, though medium-grain couscous offers more texture in the warm milk.

| | |
|---|---|
| 1 | cup medium-grain couscous (about 6 ½ ounces) or 3 cups cooked couscous |
| 4 | cups whole milk |
| 3 | tablespoons sugar |

Salt

Ground cinnamon for dusting

If using a couscoussier, prepare the couscous according to the directions on page 166. If using precooked "instant" couscous, prepare it following the directions on page 167, but omit heating the grains in the oven.

In a saucepan over medium-high heat, bring the milk to a simmer, stirring so that it does not stick to the bottom. Stir in the sugar and a pinch of salt.

Prepare 4 soup or café au lait bowls and divide the couscous evenly among them.

Remove the milk from the heat and pour over the couscous. Dust with cinnamon and serve warm on the side with a bowl of sugar for those who want it sweeter.

# Mediterranean Spice Box: A Compendium of Herbs and Spices

**ALEPPO SPICE BLEND:** A Syrian blend of six or seven spices, often including sweet and hot peppers, cinnamon, clove, cardamom, nutmeg, and sometimes ginger.

**ALLSPICE:** This dried and ground brown berry is a key spice in Turkey, Lebanon, and Syria. It frequently gives a piquant warmth to Turkish dolmas and pilafs.

**BAHARAT:** This spice mix changes with its origin. In Lebanon and Syria, it often includes allspice, black pepper, cinnamon, and nutmeg; in Egypt, it's bay leaves, black pepper, cumin, cinnamon, cloves, and nutmeg.

**BASIL:** Few combinations are more classic—or perfect—than basil and tomato. A commonly used fresh herb in the Italian kitchen, it's best shredded (cutting makes it darken quicker) and added at the last moment, as the delicate aroma dissipates quickly.

**BAY LEAVES:** Along with garlic, one of the ancient aromas of the Mediterranean kitchen. It's generally used dried, which is slightly less bitter than fresh. Used in soups, stews, and bean dishes, and with lamb and fish. Use in moderation; the flavor strengthens with cooking. Mediterranean bay leaves (usually produced in Turkey) tend to be smaller and sweeter than their Californian counterparts.

**CARAWAY:** These ribbed, crescent-shaped seeds are nutty, warm, robust, and slightly pungent with a hint of anise. A defining flavor of Tunisian cooking (often added with garlic; usually in dishes that don't include meat) and key ingredient in *tabil* spice blend and harissa.

**CARDAMOM:** These pale green pods need to be slightly crushed to release their intense, zesty sweetness. Used not only in sweet cooking, but in many savory dishes across North Africa and the eastern Mediterranean.

**CELERY:** Celery is treated like an herb in much of the Mediterranean. In Italy it's often incorporated into the sofrito, while in Spain it flavors stocks and soups. Trim the bottom white part but use the leaves.

**CHILI:** There are numerous types and heat levels of ground chili pepper. In Spain, the most common is sweet pimentón (see page 210), while in Italy, hot peperoncino gets more popular the farther south you travel. In North Africa, *piment doux* (sweet paprika) and *piment fort* (cayenne pepper) are often used together, their proportions depending on the dish or palate of the cook.

**CILANTRO:** *see Coriander*

**CINNAMON:** Hot and sharp with a sweet aftertaste. Frequently found in sweet dishes, cinnamon—both ground and in sticks (quills)—also flavors savory dishes in North Africa, Turkey, Greece, and occasionally Italy.

**CLOVE:** These dried, unopened buds are used mostly in sweet dishes, though in the eastern Mediterranean they often appear in savory dishes and tomato sauces.

**CORIANDER:** Both the seeds (as a spice) and the leaves (as a fresh herb, commonly called *cilantro* in English) are used. Dried seeds are mild and slightly pungent, with a hint of anise and a vaguely sweet aftertaste. Dry-roasting them before grinding brings out more complex flavors. Cilantro is a key herb in North Africa and often coupled with fresh parsley. Store cilantro standing upright in a glass of water in the refrigerator. One bunch yields about 1/2 cup chopped.

**CUMIN:** Finely ridged and slightly curved pale brown seeds with an earthy-warm, haylike aroma when crushed or ground and an equally earthy-warm though slightly bitter taste. (Dry-roasting makes cumin less bitter.) An essential spice in Morocco and Tunisia; in Egypt and Crete, it has been used since ancient times to season fish.

**DILL:** Especially important in Turkish and Greek cooking, fresh dill is found in soups and stews, salads, stuffings, and pilafs. Because it rapidly loses its fragrance, fresh dill should be added at the end of cooking.

**FENNEL:** Both the foliage and the bulb (heart) of fresh fennel are used; the anise flavor pairs well with fish. Fennel seeds are aromatic, sweet, and aniselike; dry-toasting heightens these characteristics.

**FENUGREEK:** These brownish pelletlike seeds have a lovely sugary, nutty taste, which is emphasized when dry roasted. But if over-roasted, or overused, the flavor becomes extremely bitter.

**GARLIC:** There are two types of dried Mediterranean garlic: common white heads and small pink ones that are more intensely fragrant. When buying, look for compact heads heavy for their size; avoid those that have excessively dry outer papers, green sprouts, or are yellowish. One head contains 12 to 15 cloves. To peel a clove, press down on the side with the heel of your hand or the flat of a knife until the skin breaks; remove. Cut out any center green part. Store in a dry, cool place.

**GINGER:** Used in dried, ground form in the Mediterranean. Ginger's tangy cross of sweetness and biting hotness shows up in many savory Moroccan dishes.

**HARISSA:** Tunisian ground chile paste; see page 165.

**MASTIC:** Amber-colored crystalline "tears" that come from the resin of a tree native to the Greek island of Chios, just off the Turkish coast near Izmir. The flavor is piney with metallic, mineral overlays. It acts as a natural thickening agent and gives a chewiness to Turkish rice puddings and Egyptian soups, broths, stews, and rice dishes. Store mastic tears in the freezer; remove and crush in a mortar with a little bit of sugar to ease pounding and to form a powder before adding.

**MINT:** In the kitchen, mint is nearly always the spearmint variety. Dried mint is important to the savory cooking of Greece, Turkey, Cyprus, and Syria, while fresh is more popular in North Africa. Store fresh mint standing upright in a glass of water in the refrigerator.

**NUTMEG:** A strong, sweet spice, nutmeg is found in various savory dishes in Italy and is often included in North African spice blends. Buy whole and grate as needed.

**ORANGE BLOSSOM WATER:** Distilled essence of bitter orange blossoms. Popular in North Africa, where it's called *zhar* or by its French name *eau de fleur d'oranger*. Potent, especially to those unaccustomed to its flavor; use with extreme moderation.

**OREGANO:** Dense and slightly sharp flavored. One of the most important and widespread herbs in Greek cooking. Generally used in dried form.

**PARSLEY:** Fresh flat-leaf parsley is probably the most popular fresh herb in the Mediterranean. In Spain, *perejil* (*julivert* in Catalan)—offered free at butchers', fishmongers', and vegetable stands—is often pounded in a picada with almonds and garlic and stirred into a dish at the end of cooking, while in Italy *prezzemolo* is cooked into the sofrito as well as added at the end. Greeks use it in everything but sweets, while Moroccans often pair it with cilantro. One bunch yields about $\frac{1}{2}$ cup chopped. Store standing upright in a glass of water in the refrigerator.

**PIMENTÓN:** Silky, brick red, and smoky-hued Spanish paprika. The peppers are dried and then slowly smoked over oak logs in carefully controlled, low-slung smoke-houses before being milled. Sweet (*dulce*), bittersweet (*agridulce*), and hot (*picante*) varieties; *dulce* is by far the most common.

**RAS EL HANOUT:** Spicy, robust, and floral, Morocco's most celebrated spice blend translates loosely to "best of the shop" and can comprise more than twenty different ingredients, including cinnamon, ginger, cardamom, nutmeg, cumin, cloves, coriander, saffron, turmeric, allspice, black pepper, cayenne, paprika, fenugreek, aniseed, lavender, thyme, mace, and dried rosebuds.

**ROSEBUDS:** Rarely used alone, dried rosebuds are crushed and blended with other spices to give a fragrant, floral component to mixes such as ras el hanout and *baharat*.

**ROSEMARY:** This piney, strong herb is widespread around the Mediterranean. It pairs particularly well with roasted lamb.

**ROSEWATER:** Another potent and popular essence in North Africa, where it's called *ma ouard* or, in French, *eau de rose*, and added to sweet dishes, pastries, and rice puddings. Use in extreme moderation if unaccustomed to the taste.

**SAFFRON:** Grown in a small number of places around the Mediterranean, the best saffron comes from the central Spanish region of La Mancha, where the hot summers and cold winters give the color strength and the aroma pungency. It take about 70,000 flowers to yield one pound of saffron. Avoid buying powder (which might be adulterated) and choose threads that range in color from deep reds to purples. To maximize saffron's culinary potential, the threads need to be briefly dry roasted and crumbled. Alternatively, soak them in a glass of warm water for 20 to 30 minutes before incorporating the liquid into the dish.

**SUMAC:** The lemony chili-flavored, maroon-red sumac is a key spice in Turkey, Syria, and Lebanon, where it's often found on the table beside salt. Used as a natural souring agent before lemons were introduced into the region, sumac is added these days for its pleasing, tangy kick.

**TABIL:** A hot Tunisian spice blend that often includes coriander, caraway, chili pepper, cinnamon, garlic, and salt.

**THYME:** One of the principal (and most fragrant) herbs in the region, it's usually used dried and often in combination with other herbs—in Tunisia with rosemary, in Italy with rosemary and bay leaf.

**TURMERIC:** Related to ginger, turmeric root is dried and grated. The inexpensive powder gives food an appealing natural mustard-yellow color. It's not a perfect substitute for saffron as the flavor is coarser and slightly pungent.

**ZA'ATAR:** A typical spice blend in Lebanon and Syria with thyme, sumac, and sesame seeds.

# Sources

Casa Oliver
(888) 807-7246
www.casaoliver.com

A Seattle-based Web purveyor of fine Spanish foods.

Dean & DeLuca
(800) 221-7714
www.deandeluca.com

The perfect place to find kitchen tools and cookware and to stock the Mediterranean pantry.

Fante's Kitchen Wares Shop
(800) 443-2683
www.fantes.com

An old and distinguished specialist cookware shop that sells every pot, pan, or tool needed in the kitchen, including paella pans and couscoussiers.

Kalustyan's
(800) 352-3451
www.kalustyans.com

Opened in 1944, this New York City emporium of spices and imported foodstuffs carries everything from various types of couscous and fregola to Calasparra rice and Camargue red rice.

La Tienda
(800) 710-4304
www.tienda.com

Specializing in Spanish goods, La Tienda offers a wide selection of paella pans, cazuelas, and imported Iberian foods, including Bomba and Calasparra rice.

Mustapha's Moroccan
(800) 481-4590
www.mustaphas.com

A Seattle-based mail-order supplier of Moroccan goods, including their own line of spices and preserved lemons.

PaellaPans.com
(718) 507-1620
www.paellapans.com

Online specialist retailer of paella pans, gas burners, leg supports, and fire stands.

Sahadi's
(718) 624-4550
www.sahadis.com

This Brooklyn store, specializing in Middle Eastern and North African products, carries various types of couscous, including Dari brand barley.

Shamra
(301) 942-9726
www.shamra.com

A Maryland-based supplier of Greek, Turkish, and Middle Eastern products, including allspice and mastic.

Spanish Table
(206) 682-2827
www.spanishtable.com

The best source for Spanish foodstuffs and materials, from paella pans to pimentón and preserved snails. Stores in Seattle, San Francisco, and Santa Fe.

Spice House
(312) 274-0378
www.thespicehouse.com

Every spice you need can be found here. Look for hand-blended Middle Eastern and North African spice mixes, from baharat to ras el hanout. Stores in Chicago and Evanston, IL, and Milwaukee.

Sur la Table
(800) 243-0852
www.surlatable.com

Excellent cookware and cookbook selection, with specialty and imported food items as well.

## Taste of Turkey.com
www.tasteofturkey.com

Online store based in McLean, Virginia, selling a wide range of Turkish and Mediterranean products.

## Tulumba
(866) 885-8622
www.tulumba.com

Mega mail-order store for all things Turkish, including Baldo and broken rice.

## Whole Foods Market
www.wholefoodsmarket.com

An excellent grocery chain to find rabbit, duck, squab, monkfish, and so on, as well as imported Mediterranean products from pastas to risotto rices.

## Williams-Sonoma
(877) 812-6235
www.williams-sonoma.com

A large and complete cookware store carrying everything from couscoussiers to paella pans.

## Zingerman's
(888) 636-8162
www.zingermans.com

Legendary Ann Arbor delicatessen and mail-order emporium that sells hard-to-find important products, including Principato de Lucedio rice, Camargue red rice, and fregola (spelled at Zingerman's as fregula).

# Select Bibliography

Abdennour, Samia. *Egyptian Cooking: A Practical Guide.* New York: Hippocrene, 2001.

Adele di Leo, Maria. *La cucina di pesce siciliana.* Rome: Tascabili Economici Newton, 2002.

Agulló, Ferran. *Llibre de la cuina catalana.* Barcelona: Lliberia Puig i Alfonso, 1933.

D'Alba, Tommaso. *La cucina siciliana di derivazione araba.* Palermo (Sicily): Vittoriette, 1980.

Alexiadou, Vefa. *Greek Cuisine.* Athens: Vefa Alexiadou, 2003.

Alford, Jeffrey, and Naomi Duguid. *Seductions of Rice.* New York: Artisan, 1998.

Algar, Ayla. *Classic Turkish Cooking.* New York: Harper Perennial, 1991.

Allotta, Alba. *I sapori del mare: Cuscus e ricette siciliane di pesce.* Trapani (Sicily): Coppola, 2004.

Andrews, Colman. *Catalan Cuisine.* Boston: Harvard Common, 1988.

Bar Pinotxo. *Pinotxo.* Barcelona: Viena, 2004.

Barrenechea, Teresa. *The Cuisines of Spain.* San Francisco: Ten Speed, 2005.

Barron, Rosemary. *Flavors of Greece.* Northampton (Massachusetts): Interlink, 2004.

Benayoun, Aline. *Casablanca Cuisine: French North African Cooking.* London: Serif, 1998.

Bennani-Smirès, Latifa. *La cuisine marocaine.* Casablanca: Al Madariss, 2004.

———. *Les Saveurs d'Algérie.* Paris: Bachari, 2002.

Bittman, Mark. *Fish: The Complete Guide to Buying and Cooking.* New York: Hungry Minds, 1994.

Bouayed, Fatima-Zohra. *Le livre de la cuisine d'Algérie.* Algiers: ENAG, 2005.

Boubezari, Karimène. *Ma cuisine algérienne.* Aix-en-Provence: Édisud, 2002.

Boucherite, Madame L. *Le guide du cuisinier algérien.* Algiers: Baghdadi, 2003.

Bouhamed, Mme. *Cuisine Kabyle: Les spécialités montagnardes inconquises.* Algiers: Les Editions El Manel, 2003.

Bsisu, May S. *The Arab Table: Recipes and Culinary Traditions.* New York: William Morrow, 2005.

Certain, Christophe. *Cuisine pied-noir.* Aix-en-Provence: Édisud, 2001.

Chalendar, Pierrette. *Cuisine de Camargue: entre Delta du Rhône et Méditerranée.* Nîmes (France): Lacour, 2006.

Chatto, James, and W. L. Martin. *A Kitchen in Corfu.* London: Weidenfeld and Nicolson, 1993.

Correnti, Pino. *Cuscus: storia, ricette, tradizioni.* Palermo (Sicily): Dario Flaccovio, 2002.

Cremona, Matty. *A Year in the Country: Life and Food in Rural Malta.* Malta: Proximus, 2003.

Crescimanno, Adele. *Old Sicilian Cooking.* Translated by Gillian Wise. Palermo (Sicily): Dario Flaccovio, 2004.

Davidson, Alan. *The Oxford Companion to Food.* Oxford: Oxford University Press, 1999.

———. *The Tio Pepe Guide to the Seafood of Spain and Portugal.* Málaga (Spain): Santana, 2002.

Eren, Neset. *The Art of Turkish Cooking.* New York: Hippocrene, 1993.

Fàbrega, Jaume. *El gran llibre de la cuina de les àvies.* Barcelona: Magrana, 2005.

———. *Traditional Catalan Cooking.* Translated by Paul Martin. Barcelona: La Magrana, 1997.

Farah, Madelain. *Lebanese Cuisine.* New York: Thunder's Mouth, 2001.

Ferrero, Aldo (editor) et al. *Risografia: Un viaggio tra passato e presente.* Vercelli (Italy): Mercurio, 2007.

Gamulin Gama, Nikica. *Croatian Cookbook.* Translated by Kristina Mestrov. Split (Croatia): Marjan Tisak, 2006.

George, Nora. *Nora's Recipes from Egypt.* Clovis (California): Self-published, 1995.

Gobert, E. G. *Usages et rites alimentaires des Tunisiens.* (Facsimile of original 1940 edition). Tunis: Sahar, 2003.

Goldstein, Joyce. *Italian Slow and Savory.* San Francisco: Chronicle Books, 2004.

———. *The Mediterranean Kitchen.* New York: William Morrow, 1989.

———. *Sephardic Flavors: Jewish Cooking of the Mediterranean.* San Francisco: Chronicle Books, 2000.

Guinaudeau, Madame. *Traditional Moroccan Cooking: Recipes from Fez.* Translated by J. E. Harris. London, Serif: 2003.

Gürsoy, Deniz. *Turkish Cuisine in Historical Perspective.* Translated by Dr. Joyce H. Matthews. Istanbul: Oglak, 2006.

Hadj Hammou, Zuleikha. *Le livre de la cuisine algérienne.* Alger (Algeria): Editions Mimouni, 1991.

Hal, Fatema. *The Food of Morocco.* Singapore: Periplus, 2002.

Hazan, Marcella. *Essentials of Classic Italian Cooking.* New York: Alfred A. Knopf: 2005.

Helou, Anissa. *Lebanese Cuisine.* London: Grub Street, 1997.

Hemphill, Ian. *Spice Notes: A Cook's Compendium of Herbs and Spices.* Sydney: Macmillan, 2000.

Jenkins, Nancy Harmon. *The Essential Mediterranean.* New York: HarperCollins, 2003.

Jerro Gerbino, Virginia, and Philip M. Kayal. *A Taste of Syria.* New York: Hippocrene, 2003.

Kaak, Zeinab. *La Sofra: Cuisine tunisienne traditionnelle.* Tunis: Cérès Editions, 1995.

Kochilas, Diane. *The Food and Wine of Greece.* New York: St. Martin's, 1990.

———. *The Glorious Foods of Greece.* New York: William Morrow, 2001.

Koehler, Jeff. *La Paella: Deliciously Authentic Rice Dishes from Spain's Mediterranean Coast.* San Francisco: Chronicle Books, 2006.

Kouki, Mohamed. *Tunisian Gastronomy.* Translated by Najoua Kouki. Tunis: Wafa, 2000.

Lladonosa i Giró, Josep. *El gran llibre de la cuina catalana.* Barcelona: Empúries, 1991.

Luján, Néstor. *Diccionari Luján de gastronomia catalana.* Barcelona: La Campana, 1990.

March, Lourdes. *El libro de la paella y de los arroces.* Madrid: Alianza, 1985.

*Medina Project.* www.medinaproject.net.

Mehdawy, Magda. *My Egyptian Grandmother's Kitchen.* Cairo: American University of Cairo, 2006.

Millo, Lorenzo. *Cocina Valenciana.* León (Spain): Everest, 2000.

———. *La gastronomía de la Comunidad Valenciana.* Valencia: Prensa Valenciana, 1992.

Montigny, Rose. *Cuisine sans souci: 1400 recettes de cuisine familiale et pratique.* Paris: Bouquins, 1973.

Morganti, Paola, and Chiara Nardo. *Il riso: La storia, le tradizioni e le ricette*. Verona (Italy): Morganti, 2004.

Morse, Kitty. *Couscous: Fresh and Flavorful Contemporary Recipes*. San Francisco: Chronicle Books, 2000.

Morsy, Magali. *Recetas a base de couscous*. Barcelona: Parsifal, 1999.

Norman, Jill. *Herbs & Spices: The Cook's Reference*. New York: DK, 2002.

Oliva, Pietro, and Maria Giovanna Poli. *Cucina sarda*. Florence: Giunti Editore, 2007.

Paradissis, Chrissa. *The Best Book of Greek Cookery*. Athens: Efstathiadis, 2001.

Petràs, Llorenç. *La millor cuina dels bolets*. Barcelona: Empúries, 2000.

Petroni, Paolo. *Il libro della vera cucina fiorentina*. Florence: Casa Editrice Bonechi, 1974.

Pilati, Giacomo, and Alba Allotta. *Cucina trapanese e delle isole*. Rome: Franco Muzzio, 2004.

Prádanos, Jorge, and Pedro Gómez Carrizo. *El gran diccionario de cocina*. Barcelona: RBA Libros, 2003.

Queralt Tomás, M. Carmen. *La cuina de les Terres de l'Ebre*. Valls (Spain): Cossetània, 2000.

Reboul, J.-B. *La cuisinière provençale*. Marseille: Tacussel, 1897.

Rezki, Mokhtaria. *Le couscous algérien*. Algiers: ENAG, 2003.

*Ricette di osteria e genti di Sicilia*. Bra (Italy): Slow Food Editore, 2003.

Riera, Ignasi. *Diccionari de la cuina catalana*. Barcelona: Edicions 62, 2002.

Roden, Claudia. *Arabesque: A Taste of Morocco, Turkey, and Lebanon*. New York: Alfred A. Knopf, 2006.

———. *The New Book of Middle Eastern Food*. New York: Alfred A. Knopf, 2000.

Salaman, Rena. *The Greek Cook: Simple Seasonal Food*. London: Aquamarine, 2001.

Seijo Alonso, Francisco G. *La cocina alicantina*. Alicante (Spain): Instituto de Estudios Alicantinos, 1973.

Taylor Simeti, Mary. *Sicilian Food: Recipes from Italy's Abundant Isle*. London: Grub Street, 1999.

Tovar, Rosa. *Arroces*. Madrid: El País Aguilar, 2003.

Vázquez Montalbán, Manuel. *La cocina catalana*. Barcelona: Península, 1979.

Vergara, Antonio. *Anuario gastronómico de la Comunidad Valenciana*. Valencia (Spain): Gratacels, 2005.

Wolfert, Paula. *Couscous and Other Good Food from Morocco*. New York: Harper & Row, 1973.

Woodward, Sarah. *The Ottoman Kitchen: Modern Recipes from Turkey, Greece, the Balkans, Lebanon, Syria and Beyond*. New York: Interlink, 2001.

Wright, Clifford A. *A Mediterranean Feast*. New York: William Morrow, 1999.

———. *Cucina Paradiso: The Heavenly Food of Sicily*. New York: Simon & Schuster, 1992.

———. *Mediterranean Vegetables*. Boston: Harvard Common, 2001.

Wright, Jeni. *The Cook's Encyclopedia of Pasta*. New York: Hermes House, 2002.

Yerasimos, Marianna. *500 Years of Ottoman Cuisine*. Translated by Sally Bradbrook. Istanbul: Boyut, 2005.

# Index

# Table of Equivalents

The exact equivalents in the following table have been rounded for convenience.

## Liquid/Dry Measures

| U.S. | Metric |
|---|---|
| ¼ teaspoon | 1.25 milliliters |
| ½ teaspoon | 2.5 milliliters |
| 1 teaspoon | 5 milliliters |
| 1 tablespoon (3 teaspoons) | 15 milliliters |
| 1 fluid ounce (2 tablespoons) | 30 milliliters |
| ¼ cup | 60 milliliters |
| ⅓ cup | 80 milliliters |
| ½ cup | 120 milliliters |
| 1 cup | 240 milliliters |
| 1 pint (2 cups) | 480 milliliters |
| 1 quart (4 cups, 32 ounces) | 960 milliliters |
| 1 gallon (4 quarts) | 3.84 liters |
| 1 ounce (by weight) | 28 grams |
| 1 pound | 454 grams |
| 2.2 pounds | 1 kilogram |

## Length

| U.S. | Metric |
|---|---|
| ⅛ inch | 3 millimeters |
| ¼ inch | 6 millimeters |
| ½ inch | 12 millimeters |
| 1 inch | 2.5 centimeters |

## Oven Temperatures

| Fahrenheit | Celsuis | Gas |
|---|---|---|
| 250 | 120 | ½ |
| 275 | 140 | 1 |
| 300 | 150 | 2 |
| 325 | 160 | 3 |
| 350 | 180 | 4 |
| 375 | 190 | 5 |
| 400 | 200 | 6 |
| 425 | 220 | 7 |
| 450 | 230 | 8 |
| 475 | 240 | 9 |
| 50 | 260 | 10 |